TRANS-ATLANTIC TRIMARAN

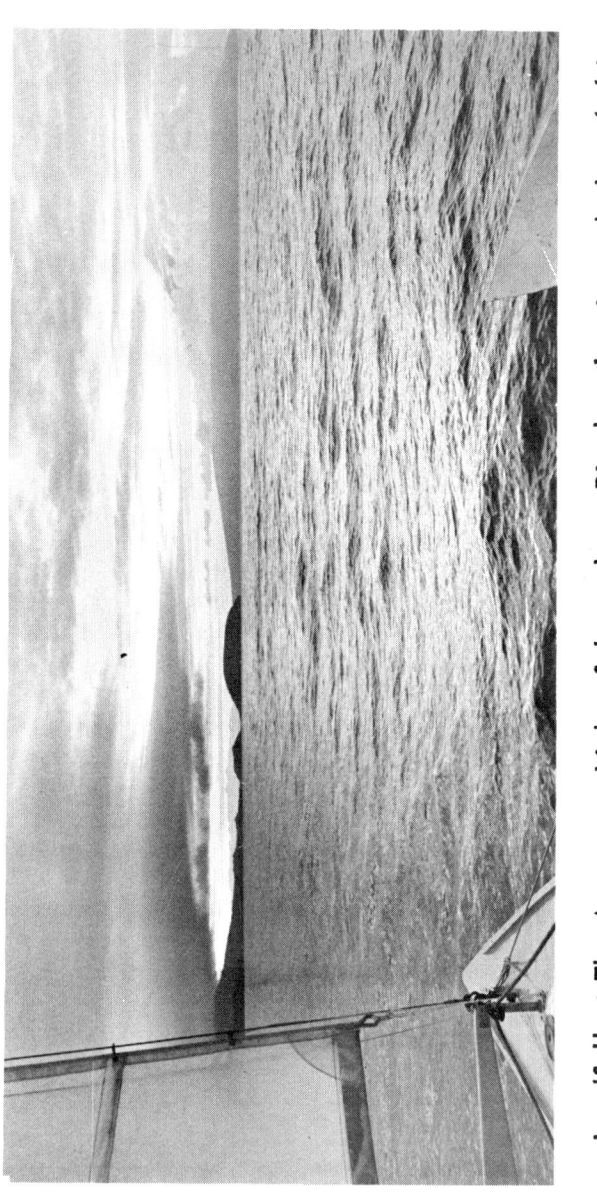

Landfall at The Azores. Light of dawn shows Pico's volcanic peak shrouded in mist, while the Port of Horta on the Island of Fayal lies just beyond mound in center of photograph.

TRANS-ATLANTIC TRIMARAN

by Arthur Piver

With a FOREWORD by Dr. JOHN MORWOOD, Founder,
Amateur Yacht Research Society

Photographic Typography by John Minges,
San Francisco

Third Printing

First Printed 1961

Published By: PI-CRAFT

50 Marlin Avenue   Mill Valley   California

TRANS-ATLANTIC TRIMARAN

FOREWORD

Most yachtsmen get the pleasure of yachting simply by commanding their little ships. A yacht is like an orchestra or an army, composed of different parts all of which seem to have their individualities which could produce disharmony in the whole. It is the commander of the yacht who keeps all these unruly parts working together to produce a simple machine which is amazingly complex in its action in converting the force of the wind into motion.

The commander of a sailing yacht at sea can achieve an immense sense of power. He is no longer weak in proportion to the forces of Nature but at times immensely strong. His personality expands to the full extent of his boat in a complete way not found in any other vehicle because he knows and understands every corner of his craft. The owner or driver of a machine with an engine, be it on land or sea can know exactly what happens to produce motion in his vehicle but he must always remember that he has frequently to refer to outside help for his fuel and engine maintenance. The sailing ship owner is free from this dependence. Once his craft is complete and well found, he needs no base and can sail around the world should he want to without refueling his craft.

The majority of yachtsmen buy their boats according to their means and fancy but certain independently minded people build their own from

2 FOREWORD

plans or kits of parts sold by yacht designers and commercial firms. Still others are yet more independent and design their boats as well as building them, preferring to feel that they are the complete owners not only of the boat but its design and construction. Such boats, if amateur designed and built, can even be slower than the professionally produced craft but their owners will still achieve the supreme satisfaction of sailing a boat which is really their own in every sense of the word. Undoubtedly, they are the elite of sailors and achieve the utmost pleasure from sailing.

The description of the trans-Atlantic crossing in this book to which I have the honour of writing this foreword is perhaps a small window into the mind of an amateur yachtsman who has achieved his supreme triumph. Arthur Piver has been designing and building boats for some years in a never ending stream, trying to develop a seaworthy craft which an amateur can make within a fairly short space of time at reasonable expense and which can develop greater speeds than the conventional ballasted yacht. To my way of thinking, Arthur reached his immediate goal of the best possible trimaran configuration in his 24 ft. NUGGET which is a fully seaworthy boat which has been sailed hard in the Pacific Ocean. But NUGGET is rather small for a passage across an ocean so NIMBLE, which is 30 ft. long, was designed and built, it being generally accepted that 30 ft. is the shortest boat capable of being comfortable in deep sea conditions yet not too big for easy handling.

In 1955 some of us started the Amateur Yacht Research Society to study everything about boats

3 FOREWORD, TRANS-ATLANTIC TRIMARAN

which, as we say, are "propelled by wind, power or human agency." At about this time, the first really good and fast catamarans were beginning to appear and among other facets of yachting, we studied these as completely as we could. But anyone who studies catamarans immediately finds that all the native peoples of the Pacific Ocean prefer the single outrigger canoe to two canoes held apart by cross beams, though the Indonesians traditionally use a single hull with outrigger floats on both sides. A few minutes work with a pencil and paper shows us that the weight, windage and wetted surface are very much less with outrigged craft of all kinds as compared with the double hulled catamaran. The stability and safety are also greater in proportion. The studies of the A.Y.R.S. therefore very soon took us into the structure of outrigger craft of all kinds.

Before the A.Y.R.S. studies began, Woody Brown, Rudy Choy, Hugo Myers and Roland Prout were building very fast catamarans and people like Bob Harris were beginning to take an interest in their design. But the presence of publications on the subject, giving the technical details of successful designs and the principles on which it was felt that designs should be based, immediately threw open the field to many newcomers and within a very short space of time a whole host of excellent designs and catamarans were being produced in all parts of the world. Fortunately for the A.Y.R.S., enough of the new designers were public spirited enough to let us have the details of their craft to such an extent that the New York Public Library now quotes us as being the World Authority on this subject.

4 FOREWORD, TRANS-ATLANTIC TRIMARAN

As could be expected, we very soon made contact with Victor Tchetchet who had proved, as did the Pacific natives before him, that the Indonesian double outrigger, which he named the "Trimaran" was faster than a catamaran of similar hull design. And, in the summer of 1957 we made our original contact with Arthur Piver.

By 1957, Arthur had made six multihulled boats; two catamarans, a single outrigger and finally three trimarans. He attributes his primary interest in trimarans to the search for greater stability than that offered by the single outrigger. His designs are very different in conception from the trimarans of Victor Tchetchet. The main hulls had round bottoms made up of what is called "Strip Planking," above which sheet plywood was used. The floats were box shaped with flat under surfaces.

Now, at this time, we of the A.Y.R.S. had discovered that the wetted surfaces of catamarans and trimarans had to be small to get the best speeds and that neither catamaran hulls nor trimaran floats achieved anything by being of "planing" shapes. This meant that the hulls which Arthur was designing at that time were of the best possible shape, though his floats were less than the best. But we also suggested that, for amateurs using plywood, a hull section with a right angled V at the keel would not lose very much and floats with square box sections with an angle lowermost would not be bad.

With that rare stroke of real genius which is given more often to the amateur than the professional boat builder, Arthur then designed his FROLIC, which I regard as the first "perfect"

5 FOREWORD, TRANS-ATLANTIC TRIMARAN

trimaran configuration. FROLIC's main hull was composed of right angled V sections below the waterline almost to the stern where they flattened out somewhat, with almost vertical plywood sides above. The floats which were eventually found to work were long boxes with square cross sections and pointed at the forward ends. Her cost was approximately $200.

Perhaps the main discovery with FROLIC was that for the same cost, in work or money, a larger and therefore faster boat could be had with the right angled V than the more efficient strip-planked hulls which Arthur had used previously. With this discovery, the road was all set for the achievement by Arthur of his ideal boat. Indeed, FROLIC, NUGGET and the craft used in this year's trans-Atlantic crossing, NIMBLE, are boats which very many people will soon be wanting to have, though tradition dies hard and it takes time for people who are used to conventional boats to take to the type.

Since the beginning of time, sailors have been looking for the perfect boat—one which will take them anywhere they want to go with safety and speed. The Piver trimarans must be considered to be a great step forwards towards the goal of all sailors because one cannot conceive of a practical way at the moment to design the hull of a sailing boat with less resistance to the wind and water forces.

It is the lot of few people nowadays to discover or invent very much. The world has been opened up everywhere. The machines which can be devised by the simple mechanic have mostly been invented. In general, it can be said that it is only by long years of study can anyone get to the fringe of knowledge in any field with real insight into the problems facing him there. However, because sailing boats have little commercial importance and sailors are such traditionalists, it is possible still to improve them both in hulls and sails.

Arthur Piver's contribution to yachting is that he has developed day sailing craft which are fast, safe and cheap and which can easily be made by amateurs. But, in my opinion, the supreme value of his work is that he has made ocean voyaging a possibility for anyone who has the practical ability to carry it out. The best ocean voyagers have been men who built their own boats.

Dr. John Morwood

Amateur Yacht Research Society
Woodacres, Hythe, Kent
England
October 20, 1960

TRANS-ATLANTIC TRIMARAN

by Arthur Piver

Thoughts of tropic nights, girl-infested islands, blue lagoons and cloud-flecked, azure skies are surprisingly easy to conjure, especially when they are related to a new sailboat which would shortly be built—except that for some reason it was more than difficult to get started on the actual construction.

This hesitation might seem strange when our activities immediately prior to this latest dream are considered—an almost frantic five-year round of building boats, sailing them, and when their features were proven, building yet another, for one thing in boat design inevitably leads to something else.

Our concern was with ancient-yet-new concepts of sailing, based on the speedy outrigger and multihulled craft which had been thoroughly proven at sea by daring and skillful sailors thousands of years previously, but which, when built and rigged with modern materials, seemed to reveal completely new vistas of safety, comfort, and speed.

It was an exciting, challenging activity—in a world in which greater and greater specialization is necessary in order to advance, we had discovered a realm in which anyone with the feeling and initiative could participate. Art rather than science—all this affiliated with the most beautiful and most nearly alive of all man's functional creations—the sailboat.

Not just any sailboat, but rather, ones which were buoyant, alive, vital—no excess weight, no limit to speed, no limit to enjoyment.

We had built and sailed a succession of small day‑sailing types; single‑outriggers, double-outriggers (trimarans), and twin hulled (catamaran).

Each kind had its advantages and disadvantages, and as the boats became larger, we decided that the most logical design for cruising sailboats was the trimaran (double-outrigger).

Primary reason for this choice was, naturally, safety. As the trimaran heels, the depressed float fights to regain the surface and thus right the boat. This it will do clear past the point where the wind spills out of the sails, whereas other multi-hulled types are liable to capsize.

Besides the primary aspect of safety, the trimaran is naturally more maneuverable, as it pivots on but a single central hull while turning, as the floats are then unweighted. Besides, it is relatively cheap to construct, and can be foldable and can therefore be trailed, even though comparatively large.

We had progressed through six trimarans, in assorted sizes, and the latest creation was the first one large enough to be seriously considered as a cruising type—it was twenty-four feet in length, and bore the valuable name of NUGGET. Some considered it a strange choice with which to christen a boat, as it may be the first time that

3 TRANS-ATLANTIC TRIMARAN

such a buoyant object was named after a rock! However, we felt the appellation consistent with our regard for this craft—a small object of great worth. As for the rock connotation—this boat could not sink, as it was constructed entirely of wood, with no ballast.

Ballast in sailboats has for hundreds of years been considered an indispensable part of such vessels, and the mere thought of one without it is difficult for the average sailor to imagine. However, we had become convinced that the stability ordinarily conferred by ballast could be improved upon by live buoyancy instead of dead weight.

And so—our NUGGET had proven herself on the gusty reaches of San Francisco Bay, and indeed even much farther, as her owner transported himself and his wife down the California Coast to Acapulco, Mexico.

Why does a man commit himself to a relatively tiny, largely untried boat on the limitless expanse of moody ocean? The sea is a stern playmate— who also makes all the rules. These laws are relatively constant, however, and when the sailor realizes that no mistake by himself or his equipment will be tolerated, on the pain of extermination—he is then ready for step number two; the choice of his boat.

In light of the foregoing, it can be seen that this is a serious matter, indeed. On one hand there is the conventional cruising sailboat. This has been proven over centuries of use and the conquest of countless ocean miles.

This, then, is the apparent logical choice, even though it is slow of gait, uncomfortable of motion, and to the person of modest means, prohibitively expensive.

In this particular case, however, our man, Jim Brown, had been exposed to the possibilities of the new outrigger type, and had built and owned one of the tiny sixteen-foot versions.

The following eposide will reveal why he had confidence in this boat, and will, incidentally, indicate the type character who is attracted to such craft.

One stormy day Jim was looking along the waterfront, his eyes lighting up as he spied the Designer coming along. "Say," he said, "you're just the fellow I'm looking for. I want to go for a sail in my little FROLIC, and can't even get it out of the slip!"

The reason was obvious. It was blowing about fifty knots, and the combined effort of two strong men was insufficient to push the boat into the wind, clear of the piles and floats comprising its berth.

They finally succeeded during a lull, and away went our hero, having a wonderfully exciting sail in conditions which would have been hazardous, if not impossible, in ordinary craft.

At a small fraction of the cost of an ordinary boat loaded with ballast, he later constructed his NUGGET, sailing over the horison, bearding the stern lord of the sea in his own abode—fulfilling his own destiny, which was to be a MAN. His voyage was a success.

And now we return to the period of dreaming of those girl-infested islands, for the logical successor to our Mexico-bound boat was her larger sister.

5 TRANS-ATLANTIC TRIMARAN

But how much larger? This question was resolved in an exciting manner by announcement by the Slocum Society of their 1960 Single-Handed Trans-Atlantic Race. What is the Slocum Society? As the name indicates, in deference to the first solo circumnavigator in a small boat, it is an organization resolved to foster, encourage, and record such odysseys.

Surely here was a challenge no self-confident designer could ignore! This is, of course, a joke, as conventional sailboats have changed hardly at all for centuries, even though materials with which to build and equip them have been vastly improved.

And so began the designing and planning of a vessel which could be handled by one man, but would be the largest consistent with that provision.

Prospects of a successful conclusion of this scheme seemed insurmountable — questions of time, money, logistics, equipment—an apparently endless succession of hurdles—but hurdles backlit by the glow of dreams to fulfill.

Convenience and cost dictated that this craft must be constructed at home; notwithstanding lack of really adequate space, to say nothing of an infinite blizzard of sawdust working its way into every corner of the residence. This might be minimized, but it was somewhat more difficult to justify the noxious odor of the chemical fumes emanating from the glass cloth with which the hulls would be sheathed.

However, with a gracious though faintly reluctant amount of forbearance on the part of the feminine contingent, the project began on schedule.

6 TRANS-ATLANTIC TRIMARAN

We had worked out a simplified system of boat construction, whereby traditional skills were not required, enabling the craft to be built with average manual dexterity. This was due largely to the fact that sheet plywood was used almost exclusively. Because the boat had no ballast, the construction could be far simpler than it would otherwise have to be in order to support a vast amount of dead weight.

Because the finished boat with floats would be far too wide (18 feet) to trail the three miles from home to the water's edge, it was built in sections, and later assembled on the shores of San Francisco Bay.

The final work was done at the establishment of Fred Jukich, who is an old sailing pal of the Skipper's, and whose shop facilities and cheerful assistance were always available for such enterprises. Nominally a sign-painter and engraver, Fred can also be found sailing his twenty-foot trimaran, flying one of his two gliders, rowing his one-man shell, surfing, skiing, building houses, or looking after his real estate interests. The above are only his principal activities.

Launching day arrived, and accompanied by the good wishes of a group of friends assembled for the event, our new craft slid unconcernedly down the ramp, floating so lightly in her native element it appeared as if she were actually suspended slightly above the water. The Designer acted as if he had been certain all along that she would float several inches above the load water line, just where planned. She did!

Next order of business consisted of rigging and fitting out work which appeared endless because

NIMBLE looks more aircraft than boat as she heads for launching.

we were so anxious to actually sail and discover if this particular boat fulfilled all the promise which her lines and lineage indicated.

The fateful day arrived at last, and NIMBLE's keel plowed a bubbly furrow with such enthusiasm that her crew whooped in delight. Back and forth across the Bay, speeding, wheeling, strapped down and eased out, on every point of sailing she more than fulfilled every previous promise.

We were, of course, anxious to make some pure speed runs, but in the testing period encountered smooth water only once when the wind was favorable, although in this instance it was blowing only about thirty knots. NIMBLE sailed easily at twenty-four knots, without wake or fuss, with only a few bubbles to mark her passage. We realized that we had a craft which would easily do thirty knots under proper conditions.

We had two months in which to test our boat, and encountered almost every sailing condition, except outright storms. We did not get a chance to encounter any rough water in the actual sea, but inside San Francisco Bay we found plenty of wind and short, steep chop.

Ample opportunity was found to evaluate the control system of the craft, for she was arranged so that one man could steer and tend sails without leaving the central cabin. A steering wheel was used in this area, and by projecting his upper body from an adjoining hatch, the sails could be manipulated.

Because of the tremendous stability of our new boat, some means of reducing pressure on the sails and rig during hard winds had to be found.

9 TRANS-ATLANTIC TRIMARAN

We had developed an automatic-sheet release, which was based on a spring loading arrangement, and which could be set so the sails would let go at a pre-determined pressure.

Without this device, we could not have made the rig sufficiently strong to withstand heavy gusts, for whereas the ordinary boat can heel and thus relieve the pressure, our new one, which was apparently non-capsizeable, could not heel more than a few degrees at any time.

A further advantage of our automatic-release was the fitting of a trip-line, so it could be activated by an easy pull. This trip-line extended through the cabin, and if the man on watch suspected something wrong on deck, he could merely pull the emergency cord. The line also trailed astern. If one of the crew should fall overboard he could, by grasping the line, release the sails. He then would have a good chance to regain the deck unaided, via the transom steps. These last were made by fastening to the transom several heavy chest handles, mounted upside down.

As an illustration of the power which the wind develops in gusts—we could mention one particular incident. On this occasion, the weather was stormy, and we had all sail set, for this was the period in which we were seeking for any weak spot in our creation. The release-cleat was set to let go in a forty-knot wind, but as the squalls were already exceeding this figure, the main sheet was being hand held, with only the job cleated. The cleat controls both jib and mainsail, so that with only the jib pulling on it it could theoretically remain locked in gusts up to about one hundred knots.

However, we encountered a tremendous squall, of such strength the jib alone activated the cleat!

Strangely enough, on our subsequent voyage the cleat never did release, for we discovered that as soon as the weather threatened, we would reduce sail area, and regardless of the storms we later encountered, never drove the boat as hard as we did in the testing stages.

An illustration of the stability of NIMBLE occurred after we had left her at Plymouth, England, and some local sailors there were trying her out. The automatic cleat had become inoperative on our trip, due to corrosion of the temporary aluminum tension unit. We apparently did not sufficiently stress the importance of easing the sheets in heavy weather, as they just cleated everything tight, and never made any effort to relieve any pressure, regardless of the strength of the wind.

As a result of this misunderstanding, the rig started to disintegrate. Wire and fittings of the strongest steel could not stand the strain, and simply began coming all apart.

Another innovation was our remote reefing arrangement for the jib, for with our control system it was imperative that no one need go on deck in dark or stormy weather. The jib reefed in a simple manner—the halliard was slacked and double lines which ran through several blocks pulled the reefed portion down to the deck. The fact that we used horizontal battens in the sail helped contain the unused portion, which gave no evidence of flogging in even strong winds.

CHAPTER 2

In the meantime, we had been searching for an economical means of transporting NIMBLE to England, but the freight rates which were quoted were invariably greater than the amount so far expended on the entire project!

We also had an unexpected assessment. We had finally decided to disassemble the boat, pack it on a trailer, and after towing it to the East Coast, reassemble it there and sail across the Atlantic Ocean. It would be easier to find the time to accomplish this task than it would be to find the money to pay the charges asked by the steamship lines.

Several days before the boat was to be taken out of the water, a strong wind arose which blew directly against NIMBLE where she was moored alongside a husky wooden barge.

It was a hazardous berth in those conditions, so the Skipper stayed on board to keep watch over the lines. The wind seemed to ease before midnight, and he decided to go home, as everything appeared to be in good order.

On returning to the berth the next morning, a distressing sight met his shocked gaze. A line had broken, and the two vessels had crashed together for some hours in the night!

NIMBLE looked forlorn. A rear cross-arm which had been left extended beyond the side of the float to protect it had the end chewed, battered,

12 TRANS-ATLANTIC TRIMARAN

and splintered for the length of a foot. It was a gaping, sickening wound. The float, however, was hardly scratched. This had to happen when a schedule had to be maintained!

The sight of the barge, however, was even worse, for it is one thing to damage one's own property, but to destroy that of another is something else again.

The heavy barge, with its massive two-inch planking, looked as if an army detachment had been practicing anti-tank measures on it. There was a large hole (fortunately above the water line) in the side, and the decking was lifted, pried up, and splintered.

Here was a interesting comparison. Two vessels, built to diametrically-opposed principles, and the lighter had gotten all the best of the argument!

It took an hour and several scraps of plywood to repair NIMBLE. As for the barge, the bill for repairing that was awaited with trepidation, for the exchequer had already shown signs of strain—with the trip not yet started!

The bill for the barge arrived in due course—$181.20. It was a telling financial set-back.

However, action was continued. NIMBLE was pulled out of the water, and disassembled for loading on a trailer. It was remarkable how little time and effort were required to take the boat apart, compared with the care necessary for the original assembling.

Finding a crew for the trip was easy, for this boat seems to attract imaginative and resourceful

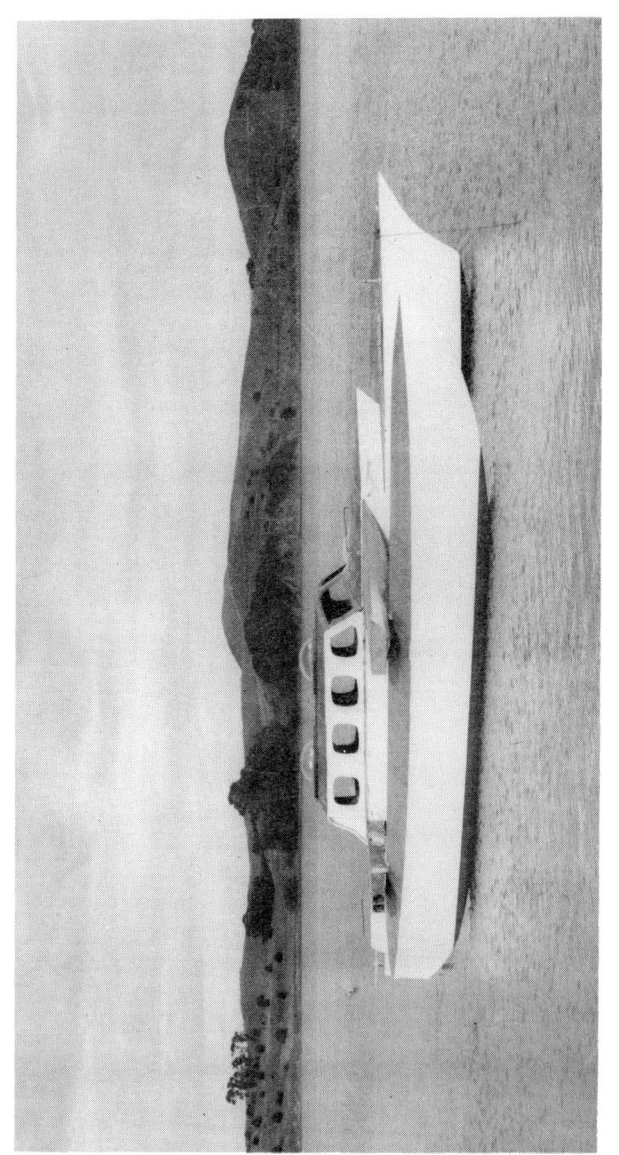

NIMBLE'S first contact with her native element.

men who contribute so much to the pleasure of sailing this type.

We had a unique clearing house for such personnel, as an organization based in England was the instrument of the meeting of a number of similarly-inclined men the world over. This was the Amateur Yacht Research Society, and its regular bulletins kept interested members abreast of all the latest sailing developments. We had a local representation of a dozen or so of these people—any one of whom would have done almost anything to be adjudged a regular crew member.

George Benello, 33, was a college instructor who was building one of our twenty-four-foot NUGGETS, even though he already owned three small sailboats. He had formerly lived in the Orient, and now wanted to return to Japan aboard his own boat. He volunteered to act as navigator. He had never navigated, but that did not bother him, as he obtained a few books and quickly taught himself the art.

The second crew member was easy to find, as we could not have kept him away at gun-point. He was Bill Goodman, 28, who later became manager of the European Division of our organization, with headquarters at Humlebaek, Denmark.

We first met over the telephone, for he had read of our activities in the bulletins of the Research Society. He called one evening from Texas, and a spirited conversation ensued. He was so interested that he called the next morning—then the following day, and the next week arrived on the scene, unable to keep himself away from such fascinating activity.

Bill had already once crossed the Atlantic—on

15 TRANS-ATLANTIC TRIMARAN

a sixty-foot ketch. After sailing on NIMBLE he became so enthusiastic that there was no stopping him. This was refreshing, for normally it is easier to change a man's religion than it is to change his ideas about boats. We usually are little concerned with established sailors, being more interested in beginners who have no prejudice to overcome, and who are not conditioned by the limitations of conventional boats.

It had been arranged to borrow a large boat trailer, and it was being surveyed in preparation to loading the boat upon it.

"It's great to have a roomy trailer like this one," exulted the Skipper, "it is certainly commodious." The more he considered it the roomier it seemed to be, so he finally measured it. It was wide, all right—too wide. Eight inches too wide for highway travel, and he had to wait until the day of departure before discovering this distressing fact!

Then ensued a council of war. After many measures and countermeasures it was decided to take two trailers; one small one owned by the Skipper, on which the two floats would travel, and a larger borrowed one, which would transport the central hull, spars, and cross-arms.

The small trailer would be towed by Bill's eleven-year-old car, for which he had paid $65. It was regarded with many misgivings, but actually ran all the way across the United States without incident.

The larger one was hooked to the Skipper's pick-up truck. The hull was so long in relation to the trailer that the bow extended far beyond the hitch. In order to make it fit, the tail gate of the truck was removed, and the bow just barely cleared the cab. The mast, which extended even beyond the bow, was well up in the air, above the truck.

Gear and supplies were loaded in the hull, and away went the rig for a test run. It was terrible— at about thirty miles per hour speed the trailer would whip dangerously from side to side, actually throwing the truck back and forth.

Gear was reloaded—conditions improved, but not nearly enough to even contemplate going any distance. And the time for departure had nearly arrived!

Once more the gear was reloaded, and after another trial it was decided that the situation was at least marginal—it would be dangerous to drive faster than about forty miles per hour, but at that speed, it might be possible to hazard the journey.

17 TRANS-ATLANTIC TRIMARAN

CHAPTER 3

And so began the Odyssey. The truck, with George and the Skipper, went first, with Bill following. A volunteer driver had been chosen to accompany Bill and help with the work, for in order to maintain the chosen schedule, we were to drive straight through to the East Coast, with stops only for food and gasoline.

We could not have been more fortunate in the choice of another hand, for the newcomer, Tony, proved invaluable. He had never even been near a sailboat before, but became so engrossed with the project that he stayed on even after we arrived at the Atlantic, working like a beaver until NIMBLE sailed away. Standing on the beach, he vowed that it would not be long until he had a similar craft of his own.

He was also a lot of fun on the trip. A Hungarian Freedom-Fighter, he had had experiences which gave him a maturity far beyond his limited number of years. He also was a virile and handsome fellow, with a huge shock of blond hair, and we used to enjoy watching the reactions of various young ladies as they first saw him. Could there be a hint of envy in his fellows? Could be, although the Skipper was two-score and ten, and had long been a married man; George was engaged; and Bill almost still a bridegroom.

One interesting thing about Tony was his awareness of bread, a quality which proved quite educational on the automobile journey, and was of subsequent value when assessing the types with which to equip our ship for voyaging. Ordinary American bread was contemptuously dismissed as unfit for human consumption, being just so much fluff, but as bread was encountered with varying qualities of taste and texture, the merits and shortcomings were pointed out.

We had planned to cross the United States on Route 40, but as there was still snow on some mountain passes when we departed on April 28, we chose the somewhat longer Route 66.

Driving the truck was an arduous chore. We were sure that if a policeman saw the manner in which the trailer swayed all over the highway, we would be summarily banished from the road. The slow speed at which we were forced to travel was so maddening, however, that we were always pushing the speed right up to the point where the swaying would commence. A cross-wind would complicate matters, for then the boat would sway at an even lower speed.

We drove in four-hour shifts. The relief driver would try to snatch some sleep while sitting on the right side of the cab, while the driver fought every second to keep the trailer from swaying and still maintain maximum speed. Bill and Tony had it easy in comparison, for not only did they have a comfortable sedan, but could use the entire back seat for relaxing when off duty.

Complications arose when we entered the State of Arizona. The checking officials insisted on a fee of $14—this occurred just after the Skipper had paid $22 for a new tire! He did some mental arithmetic and groaned inwardly. "Let's see, ten

19 TRANS-ATLANTIC TRIMARAN

states at $14 per state—that adds up to $140!" At that rate, the budget would not only be ruptured, it would be destroyed!

Arizona did have some compensations, however, for the desert scenery was entrancing if awesome, accompanied by the fluffiest white clouds in the bluest sky that any of the travelers had ever seen.

Do you know—no other state demanded a fee? That was indeed welcome, but the difference was made up in subsequent difficulties. A total of six tires had to be purchased, as well as two new trailer wheels.

However, the entire countryside was beautiful in the Springtime, and the 3,600-mile journey was a delight, regardless of the various handicaps. A perhaps portentous encounter occurred in one of the mid-West states.

"Where you goin' with that boat?" asked a farmer-type female.

"Gonna sail across the Atlantic," replied the Skipper, "want to go along as cook?"

"Not me, and you're crazy. You'll drown!"

On we pounded, finally reaching the Eastern turnpikes, of which we had heard. They were great, with mile after mile of unobstructed highway. They weren't expensive, either—that is, if you were driving passenger cars. We were towing trailers, however, as well as driving a truck, and the tolls mounted alarmingly. Also there was little choice of the make of gasoline at the various stops, and the Skipper's credit card often had to be bypassed with the use of cash, instead.

Besides other incentives to press on, we had our own slogan—"Beat the bottle!" This was a result of our having read that a bottle drifted across the North Atlantic in four months. We also used the same theme when asked how we could communicate without a radio transmitter. "Why," we would say, "we'll just send a message ahead— by bottle."

There were several incidents on the turnpikes. On one occasion, at night, the trailer was swaying all over the road, but the driver was just too tired or just too rushed to want to slow down.

He assumed that the lights just behind were Bill's as usual, but later found out that they were those of a policeman, instead!

"I was right behind that cop," reported Bill, "and was sure he was going to stop you. He must have been confused by the whole affair, for he finally pulled over to the side of the road—perhaps to mull it over. When he came up again a little later the trailer was no longer swaying, so he continued on by."

Fire aboard is one of the greatest hazards of sailing, and we experienced such a situation— although we weren't on board and we weren't sailing! Bill and Tony were driving along the turnpike when another car pulled alongside, with the driver gesticulating wildly and pointing astern. They looked back, to see billows of smoke and ugly yellow flames eating away on top of one of the floats.

Quickly stopping, they found that a discarded cigarette had landed in one of the life preservers which had been used as padding between the lashings and the float. This cost us one life preserver and a circular charred place on the pontoon about one foot across. Interestingly enough, the glass cloth was still there, although the resin which held

21 TRANS-ATLANTIC TRIMARAN

it had all burned away. A bit of resin and paint later made it as good as new.

The trip had now reached its final stages, with only two hundred miles left to go. It was night on the turnpike, and George and the Skipper were waiting at a rest stop for Bill and Tony, who had been out of sight behind for some time.

After about an hour came the word by radio from a cruising maintenance truck—the trailer had lost a wheel, and was pulled up along the roadway.

What to do? It was the middle of the night, with no possibility of any repairs until morning, so it was decided that the truck would continue on, with the car to follow when possible. There would be work to do on the central hull before the floats would be needed, anyway.

And so, the truck rolled into Swansea, Massachusetts, where arrangements had been made to assemble the boat at the facilities of Al and Wally Sunderland, who handled our products in their area. They had built a sixteen-foot trimaran for demonstration purposes, and were soon to begin construction of a twenty-four footer. It had taken us four-and-one-half days to travel 3,600 miles.

All day passed, with no word of the missing vehicles, and people began worrying. "How will you finish the boat without floats?"

The Skipper knew the qualities of the missing men, and made a little speech. "You don't know what kind of fellows these two are—they'll get those floats here if they have to carry them on their backs!" Sure enough, in they drove that night.

As for weight of equipment—it is the same story. In an ordinary boat, the fittings are always pulling against the great mass of the keel and related structure, and so must be tremendously strong. We, on the other hand, used fittings of a weight usually found on a light dinghy. Gear failure was practically unknown. For instance, we had been in such a rush to get sailing after launching NIMBLE that the main sheet blocks were merely screwed to the deck—a procedure which would have been unthinkable with a conventional boat. We had been through some fifty-knot gales with this arrangement, and had seen no sign of strain at these seemingly vulnerable points.

The lighter the gear, the lighter the price, which is a happy relationship. Part of the challenge of creating these new craft is the satisfaction of being able to do so at a fraction of the cost of the traditional type. We feel it is not much of an accomplishment to just go out and buy needed equipment—all that takes is money. To be able to build a boat without money — that is an accomplishment!

Our boat has been called the "Surplus Special," because so much of it had been purchased from the stores which feature unneeded material which originated with the Armed Forces.

These places have proven to be veritable treasure troves, and we were lucky to have lived near a metropolitan center where they are located.

Of course, some bizarre selections are apparently inevitable in such a situation. A few people had asked why we had our particular shape of glass in the cabin windows. The answer, of course, is that the Skipper had found them at Surplus, and

25 TRANS-ATLANTIC TRIMARAN

as they were of approximately the right size, and made of shatterproof glass, with a cost of but twenty-five cents each, their acquisition was a foregone accomplishment. The windshield glass in our boat was also shatterproof, and had come from an expired automobile.

Our system of life lines was unorthodox, and even though we did not expect to have to go on deck in foul conditions, we were anxious to have safeguards in this respect.

A great deal of money can be expended upon these essentials in the conventional boat, but we considered our system to be both effective and inexpensive.

Because of the narrowness of our fore and after decks, we felt that the usual fence-like life lines would not be suitable, and instead of the common vertical arrangement, we used horizontal lines.

On the outboard of our side decks we had a bridle device which held the side stays, and also acted as life lines. From the bow we had ropes splaying outboard to points on the forward cross arms, and a similar set-up aft. It was thus not too difficult to fall overboard, but the victim would probably never reach the sea, being intercepted by the horizontal lines.

We had no actual need of the lines at any time on the voyage, although at one stage, while Bill and the Skipper were doing some maintenance work on the rigging, a sea unexpectedly thundered aboard. They were both sitting on the edge of the cabin roof, however, and instinctively grabbed at the nearby bridle—each hollering for the other to hang on.

While we were at Swansea people would approach on the street and inquire about the boat and prospective journey, and also visited the scene of our labors in goodly numbers. The sea and its traditions was obviously deeply engrained in these folks—they showed much more basic interest than did the Westerners we had encountered.

A short though amusing conversation took place at the truck drivers' diner where we usually ate. The waiter had become used to us as regular customers, and finally asked a question. "Say, are you the fellows who are going to sail to England on that small boat?"

The Skipper looked at him in feigned horror: "Do we look like we're crazy?"

There was no answer. The waiter looked apologetic.

The New England hospitality was so all-embracing it was difficult to remember that we had a boat to put together.

We were staying at a cottage owned by our hosts, the Sunderlands, and found innumerable items of interest which distracted us from the tasks at hand. There were some particularly intriguing little clams we had never before seen. They lived just at the edge of the water, and were chiefly distinguished by their habit of squirting water up into the air, to a height of six inches or so. It was fun to just sit there, watching the tiny jets up and down the beach, even though the sand from the surface showed no other evidence of life.

27 TRANS-ATLANTIC TRIMARAN

One day we received a telephone call from New York, which was several hundred miles away. It was one of the officials of the Slocum Society, and he had exciting news. "Say, we have found steamer space on which to ship your boat to England, and it's free!"

The Skipper had an answer for that. "That's great, but I have two fellows here whom I have promised a sail to England, and if I try to back out now they'll KILL me."

Later we were visited by several of the Slocum luminaries, and it was interesting to meet in the flesh men with whom we had been corresponding for some time.

CHAPTER 5

Work continued apace, and on May 8 NIMBLE was once again water borne, appearing just as happy with the Atlantic brand as she had been at home.

We stepped the mast, adjusted the rigging, hoisted the sails—it was simply great to be flying along once again in that wonderfully effortless manner.

We enjoyed the reactions of people who had never before seen our boat sail. Typical comments were: "Oh, boy, look at her go!" "Must have an engine in her."

The Sunderlands are multihull sailors, and the aspect of NIMBLE's performance which most impressed them was her great maneuverability. As a matter of fact, it was this characteristic which determined her name. Although proportionately lighter than her smaller predecessors, she evidently has sufficient mass to carry her way when coming about. This she will do even in rugged going.

Representatives of a great weekly pictorial magazine spent a whole day shooting pictures and interviewing us. One of them was a well-known sailor, and he was amazed at the way NIMBLE performed.

We overheard him talking to his wife, who arrived on board later. He said excitedly—"You should see this thing go! We were passing motor

NIMBLE has a test-sail on San Francisco Bay.

boats, and there was practically no wind!"

Well, we had been passing motorboats, although they were of the small outboard variety. They had been going five or six knots, which was just about the speed of the wind at that time. NIMBLE partially fulfilled one of the Skipper's standards— that his boats would sail as fast as the wind, regardless of its strength. This she does in the lighter airs.

Our new enthusiast declared that he would soon own a similar craft. We smiled in resigned understanding, for we had heard such a statement often before. It seems that these boats are of such almost unbelievable fun to sail that after people have ridden on them and gone home, their memories fail to retain a picture sufficiently vivid to spur them on to actually building one. As a matter of fact, the diminishing of the remembered picture is one of the charms of operating this type craft; for every time you go out you discover anew the breathless fascination of high speed under sail.

The time had arrived to seriously consider the amount and kind of stores we should obtain for our journey.

One problem we had in reverse. This was medical supplies. At the beginning of the actual construction of NIMBLE the Skipper had spent some time regarding the important problem of a good medical kit. He had read lists of necessities which were published in various aids to the prospective voyager, but these invariably seemed not

31 TRANS-ATLANTIC TRIMARAN

only complete to the point of overabundance, but were obviously expensive, as well.

The different ship chandleries all had neat packaged kits, from a price of just several dollars up to about ten dollars, which seemed to be in our expenditure range.

"Well," he would think, "that three-dollar job looks pretty small, but with the budget as it is, can we afford anything more elaborate?"

The question was resolved when George's Grandmother in New York volunteered to furnish the medical kit. It was a great relief to hear of the kind offer. That was one less problem to consider.

Her generosity could only be described as overpowering. On arriving at Swansea, we were confronted with three large cardboard cartons. "What in the world is in those?"

We found out. The name of a pharmaceutical concern on the boxes gave us a clew, and when we probed, the results were astonishing. We had here enough to stock a hospital! There was everything from a small surgical kit to bottled oxygen to a bottle of pills labeled "For Brittle Bones!" The only thing we coult not find was a book of directions for do-it-yourself surgery.

"As soon as we get to sea," said the Skipper, "I will have the authority to use that surgical kit. Have any of you boys had any complaints lately?"

This question, for some reason or another, failed to evoke much enthusiasm from the crew. They were also asked to immediately report any evidence of chipping of their skulls, in deference to the pills labeled "For Brittle Bones."

We had, verily, the embarrassment of riches, for there was the stowage space for but a fraction of the available supplies. We managed to cram what we considered to be the essentials in a relatively small plastic container, leaving hundreds of dollars worth of pharmaceuticals behind.

Actual consumption of medical supplies on the trip amounted to exactly—ONE Band-Aid!

Date of departure was set for noon on May 11, and as this fateful day drew inexorably closer, the various necessities coincident with our leaving grew more urgent. We had made inquiry as to requirements in England attendant upon our being admitted there without difficulty.

One of these was the need to obtain a clearance from the health authorities. We had resigned ourselves to being measured and probed by some medical practitioner, and had driven to the Port Doctor at Fall River, which was a town adjoining Swansea, and which would be our official point of origin, as it possessed the necessary official designation.

As we sat in the doctor's waiting room, we tried each to convince the other that he should be the first to submit to the ministrations of the medical man. Our levity was quite a contrast with the mien of several people also waiting—if they had also possessed a sailboat, perhaps their health might have been sufficiently improved to eliminate the need of their presence.

When the time finally arrived, Bill and the Skipper went together—to be met by a surprise. First the doctor inquired about our projected voyage with obvious envy. It then developed that we were not the ones who needed the medical

33 TRANS-ATLANTIC TRIMARAN

clearance, but the Port of Fall River itself! We were given an impressive document stating that there were no cases of contagious disease in the area—we as individuals did not even count!

And so, that hurdle proved minuscule. A comic opera atmosphere prevailed, however, in the announcement that the port authorities insisted that we needed an anti-rat certificate as well, and we were instructed to report to the official in charge of de-ratting. In the light of our brand-new, freshly-painted nautical conveyance, this seemed preposterous, so we merely omitted obedience to these instructions.

The selection of food stocks was a subject of much discussion. It was finally decided that Bill and George would work this out in conjunction with the neighboring super-market, which they proceeded to do.

In the meantime, NIMBLE was swinging at anchor in the narrow channel nearby, and everything had to be ferried out by small boat.

This activity was somewhat handicapped by the fact that it had started to rain, and all the loading operations were carried out in these conditions.

We were lucky that we had decided to carry the water in one-gallon plastic bottles, for it would have been awkward to fill tanks so far from the source of supply. Our bottles were made of a thin but particularly tough plastic (high-density polyethelene). We had been warned they had the peculiar property of absorbing odors and tastes, and so we had to store them where there would be no bilge water or fuels. Of course, we had no place but the bilge in which to actually place them, and as the boat had not yet shown any signs of leaks, did not worry about their contents being sullied.

Supplies from the grocery store arrived in a gigantic pile—we began to wonder about a subject which had bothered us from time to time—how do you stow a significant amount of gear and supplies in a boat which is just an overgrown canoe? We had planned to use the floats for stowage space if necessary, but had not gotten around to cutting hatches in them.

Float hatches in later models of NIMBLE have been simplified, as now the floats are integral with the side decks, and by lifting a hatch on deck, the floats are readily available.

And so the food was loaded aboard. In order to keep it from getting rain-soaked, it was shoved into the cabin as soon as possible. What a sight! It almost filled the area, and as we still had not loaded personal gear, it appeared as though we had a real problem on our hands.

Although of shallow draft, NIMBLE has deep V-bottom sections, and we were surprised to find that the food stowed easily, with the cabin area being cleared in short order.

Next came clothing, bedding, etc. This really filled the cabin as it too was thrown below to escape the dampness outside. It looked as though we were going to have to make this trip on the outside—looking in!

Strangely enough, all this gear stowed with little difficulty, and although we had not had the time to catalogue the locations of various items, it practically all disappeared from the living area. We did not need the space in the floats, after all.

CHAPTER 6

There was a goodly crowd to see us off, so we were rushing to get away by our noon deadline. As a matter of fact, we had to, for there was a swift tide in our area, and what little wind there was from the SE—right in our faces.

Up went the sails, and the anchor line was shortened preparatory to getting away.

Just then NIMBLE swung in the narrow channel and lodged on a nearby sand bar. This could be embarrassing on a falling tide, but Bill jumped overboard to shove us off.

We heard gasps from the spectators, who expected him to almost disappear from sight. The advantage of a shallow draft was immediately apparent, however, as he was wet only to the knees. A shove on the bow—away we went!

Then ensued a four-hour sail to the ocean—a distance of some twenty miles. We had some practice navigating in fog, and what little we could see of the shore was bathed in misty, rainy conditions.

The Skipper was somewhat mystified when Bill insisted on shaking hands and congratulating him on their departure. Could it be possible that someone had actually doubted that the trip would not continue on schedule?

It was wonderful to be actually on our way, and the fact that we were on schedule was somewhat surprising, at that. However, we had a deadline to meet some 3,000 miles away at Plymouth, where we expected to land on approximately June 7, if all went well.

Our leaving occurred on May 11, although the actual departure for navigating purposes would be taken from the Nantucket Lightship.

We had not yet had an opportunity to swing our compass, and so had to achieve this essential ritual before we reached the actual ocean. We spent several hours in Narragansett Bay, accomplishing this task.

Daylight was fading as we slowly sailed out of the Bay into the ocean, an almost non-existent breeze allowing us to barely breast the incoming tide.

The scene was most intriguing. All about us on the shore and on rocks extending toward the water were old mansions of all degree of fanciful architecture of long ago, many with for-sale signs prominently posted. We had heard of this area as the former playground of the rich, and it was interesting to see the antique memorabilia of financial stature minus income tax.

At this time we had our first formal ship meal, and our tiny primus stove hissed cozily away, struggling with all its slight power to boil the water which would transform the awaiting packet of dried soup from a curious though pungent mass of indeterminate origin into a delicious food.

We ghosted on, and as darkness fell, we crawled by the Brenton Lightship, to be swallowed by dense fog—and calm.

All night we could hear the fog horn from the Lightship, as we strove, through watch after

37 TRANS-ATLANTIC TRIMARAN

watch, to make distance against the slight movement of air, which invariably came from the SE—dead ahead.

Our original plan had been to sail directly to the open ocean as close as possible to the opening of Narragansett Bay, and then strike directly for England over the great circle route, allowing for a detour around Newfoundland, which lay athwart our course.

Before actually departing, however, we had checked with the Weather Bureau, to be apprised of the fact that strong NW gales were then prevalent on our projected route. We were advised to sail directly East from the Nantucket Lightship, following the steamer track 1,000 miles, and then take the great circle route the balance of the journey. We were supposed to encounter prevailing SW winds upon turning North. We chose to follow this advice.

There were other complications, but apparently not serious. These involved navigational problems. Besides a surplus ($7.50) U. S. Army radio for emergency—the "Gibson Girl,"—we had a small do-it-yourself, Kit-type radio direction finder. This did not have the proper channel for receiving time ticks with which to verify our watches for determining longitude.

We had ordered a suitable radio from New York, which we had learned was available from surplus there at a reasonable price. This failed to arrive, and we received word just prior to departure that this was no longer available. Then ensued a conference. George insisted that his expensive wrist watch was highly accurate, and that he could obtain correct Greenwich time just

38 TRANS-ATLANTIC TRIMARAN

before leaving, and that should suffice.

The watch was one of the self-winding variety, and was said to be more accurate than the older type because the spring was always at a constant tension. This sounded reasonable, but when Bill and the Skipper learned that this particular timepiece would run down in five or six hours if unworn, they promised themselves that it would seldom leave George's wrist.

Actually the watch did prove itself, being surprisingly accurate, regardless of its modest dimensions.

Another factor militated in defense of our reliance on this timepiece. This was the fact that in civil broadcasting in England, the local time, which in this case is obligingly of the Greenwich Meridian, is given every hour. We could thus correct the watch by means of our little radio direction finder while still hundreds of miles from England. Time is not needed for the determination of latitude, of course, and we felt that even if we did not have accurate time, we could achieve our proper latitude while still well at sea, and merely sail East until we reached our destination.

If we could have foreseen what actually did later happen we might not have dismissed this matter so lightly, for our direction finder became inoperative right after our reaching the open sea, and our arrival at England was accompanied by such prolonged fog that we had no chance of taking sights for hundreds of miles as we approached our landfall.

However, here we were at sea South of Newport, drifting in the fog and rain. We did not know exactly where we were, but at least we did not

39 TRANS-ATLANTIC TRIMARAN

have to listen to the monotonous sound of the Brenton Lightship as we had the preceding night.

All day we floated aimlessly, and as dusk approached, we could see mistily outlined but a few feet off the port side, a low, sandy island. Just then a vicious squall swept in from the SE, and we were trapped on a lee shore—on the Nantucket Shoals.

For anyone, who for some perverse reason might wish to catalogue the world's roughest water, we are sure that this area would be near the head of the list. The waves were so steep as to be almost square, with no chance of riding over them as there were no liquid slopes to climb.

We felt lucky to be on a trimaran which did not even heel, and this great stability gave us full driving power for the sails, while the thin hulls sliced effectively through the craggy, white-capped obstacles which opposed us.

If we had not been on a lee shore we would have driven the boat in a more reserved manner, but we had no intention of ending our voyage before it had properly begun on that inhospitable sandy beach we had sighted earlier.

It was a rough, nerve-wracking experience, especially for George and the Skipper, who found themselves thoroughly seasick. George had partaken of some apparently ineffective motion pills from a handy supply, but the Skipper simply accepted the affliction as part of the price of cruising—he invariably was seasick for the first three days of any trip after having been ashore for a protracted period. It was just something temporary to endure—and ignore as much as possible.

Luckily, Bill felt fine, and as no one could

sleep in all the wild confusion of those crashing seas and screaming wind, he remained at the wheel for hours.

The storm continued unabated, but about midnight it was felt that sufficient distance to windward had been gained, so the boat was hove-to. This was interesting, as we had not previously had an opportunity to try our new craft in this classic maneuver.

The results were inconclusive, for regardless of how much the sail was reduced, that boat just wouldn't stop sailing, and was always going ahead at the rate of several knots. We did not cut down sail to the point of ridiculousness, and so on that voyage we did not really learn how little sail was necessary for the proper execution of this status. We expected to do a lot of heaving-to later, but as will be developed by our story, we discovered an entirely different way of conducting our craft in stormy conditions.

The next day broke to the old familiar calm, fog, and light rain. This was getting monotonous. We did not know where we were, as the radio direction finder refused to function. We had no depth sounder, and our pitot-type speedometer was also out of order.

To add to the confusion, ships were beginning to hoot all about us, and this is an uncomfortable experience in a boat with no way on, so it could not be maneuvered in case a sharp steel prow should suddenly rush upon us out of the whiteness of the fog—or worse, out of the blackness of the night.

We did, however, have a radar reflector in the form of our wooden mast, which had been painted with aluminum paint for just such a contingency. For several years the Skipper had quizzed various representatives of radar equipment at boat shows he visited, as to the efficacy of such an action. He never did get a satisfactory answer, but in one yachting publication had read how a suitable reflector could be made by using aluminum paint on cloth. And so, we were pretty certain we could be seen by these other boats, most of which were probably coastal steamers with radar equipment aboard. We had hoped to have a friendly soul in some harbor actually try his radar set on our mast in order to resolve this question, but had never encountered a suitable opportunity for such a test.

And so, there we were, still drifting. All that day, and all the next night. We had left Narragansett Bay on Wednesday evening of May 11, and here it was dawn of Saturday, May 14. We had already left, but had not actually departed, for Nantucket Lightship was to be our final point, as far as navigational and elapsed time was concerned.

There was a reason for our being particular about our time of departure, for although circumstances up to the present had not been propitious, there remained the possibility that we could make a fast passage. We had the fastest sailing craft ever to venture on the Atlantic, and given some good conditions from our point of departure and beyond, had the opportunity of giving a good account of ourselves. Assuredly, a small boat such as ours would require ideal conditions, but the opportunity was there.

The record across the Atlantic Ocean was held by the 185-foot schooner Atlantic, which had average some eleven knots from Sandy Hook to the Lizard in 1905.

Eleven knots! Why, our boat could go almost that fast when she was anchored! This is one of the exciting things about sailing this new type boat. Here in a tiny, inexpensive craft, we had the opportunity of beating records of mighty Clipper Ships which had had one-hundred times our sail area and one-thousand times our weight. No yachtsman in a conventional boat even dreams of such attainments, but here was our opportunity — we would grasp it if conditions permitted.

Of course, in order to obtain spectacular speed in so small a boat, the wind must come from astern or nearly astern, for these boats surf like mad down the faces of combers. When the breeze is from other points, and is of sufficient strangth to drive the boat rapidly, the ensuing sea is too large in proportion to the size of the boat to permit hight speed. Thus much larger trimarans will be required for sensational times on headings other than down-wind.

Also, the record on which we had aspirations was the result of thousands of voyages, and it was not too likely that we would meet ideal conditions the first time. Ideal conditions? A veritable joke, as you will presently see.

Anyway, here we were, sick of just drifting around, going nowhere, nothing but solid water underneath, diluted water about and above, with the dampness now being strongly felt below. We had had enough, and even though still North of our intended point of departure, we turned East toward the trackless ocean.

43 TRANS-ATLANTIC TRIMARAN

CHAPTER 7

It was a wonderful feeling to be actually heading in the right direction, even if the wind was a mere whisper, and still from the SE.

In a few hours we were out of the fog. The wind picked up somewhat, and we set the genoa, which has the generous dimensions of eighteen feet along the foot. This was great! Skies were still grey, but our spirits soared. We whooped with delight when several propoises began playing about the bows. Lucky porpoises! In ordinary boats, they have only one pair of bows by which to gambol, here in this latest type they possessed the luxury of three such assets! We feel a great kinship to these playful creatures. Happy by nature—with no apparent purpose in life! We also saw a small whale, and talked about the marine wonders we should see when we reached the prolific waters of the Gulf Stream.

And so continued this happy day—happy until midnight — when IT struck! A shuddering blast from the NW, unheralded and unwelcome; it jibed the boom with a crash, and the Skipper popped up through the helmsman's hatch like a Jack-in-the-box and let the mainsail down with a rush.

The sail was roughly furled from the main hatch, the ship headed down-wind and the jib reefed down to its fifty feet of storm area. It was evident that we were in for some nasty weather, for the wind was howling through the rigging.

The sea built up in seconds, and the boat was run off before it, with a warp dragging astern, according to current practice. We were receiving our first crucial test. You can sail around the harbor for a hundred years and still not know how your boat will act at sea—we were about to find out!

There was no sleep aboard the remainder of that night. The seas would break just astern— first there would be a hiss, followed by a tremendous crash, and the boat would jump. Then came a loud rushing noise as the foam from the breaking sea would hurtle by, with the ship trembling.

One thought was in everybody's mind—"What will happen if the seas should come from the side?" No such dire event occurred on that first night, and by the light of morning we could see our situation.

Looking astern was a frightening sight—we estimated the height of the awesome waves to be between twenty-five and thirty feet, which by rule of thumb indicated a wind of approximately twice those figures, in knots. The top five or six feet of these giants would break forward, like surf on a beach, presenting an unnerving sight as they thundered toward us.

We were watching this performance, admiring the behaviour of the boat, which had taken no solid water aboard, but still wishing we were somewhere else. After all, the boat had in the past few hours proven that giant waves were not too dangerous—we were anxious to get back on our

One of our favorite water sports—Porpoise Watching.

course, which was impossible with waves this size.

Suddenly, the warp, which had been trailing astern in a loop, became twisted on itself so that apparently its resistance was reduced—as the next sea steepened prior to breaking, the boat simply surfed ahead of it, and it broke well astern.

Delighted, we eagerly pulled in the warp and shook out the reef in the jib. After that NIMBLE surfed for hour after hour, always ahead of the break, and with no water on deck other than spray blown aboard from adjacent breaking areas.

We next discovered something even more exciting. If there was sufficient distance between trough and crest, we did not have to steer directly downwind, but could sail across the seas if our course required it.

The giant wave would well up as our tiny craft sped across its face, rising higher until the crest approached the breaking point. Away we would wheel, swooping down the wave face, headed for the safety of the trough! Every once in a while a wave would subside in a flurry of foam. NIMBLE would whisk through the disturbed white water with hardly a tremor, and as the new wave built up she would rise toward the top, and then, as danger threatened, dive again for the shelter at a lower level. We reached speeds up to twenty knots in this awesome game—under jib alone!

It was incredible—terrifying—wonderful—we had mastered Nature in one of her most vicious moods!

NIMBLE laughs at storms—for SPEED IS SAFETY.

Strangely enough, in lesser gales we had

greater problems. For instance, when the waves built up to the point where they were all breaking seas, and hence dangerous except to sail before them, we might reduce sail to jib alone.

The wave builds prior to breaking, and NIMBLE surfs readily, shooting ahead as though propelled by a giant slingshot.

In this instance, however, the crests are so close together that the boat has hardly started surfing when she slows down upon starting up the back of the wave just ahead. Almost immediately the break of the following sea arrives with a roar and a crash, and if the boat had not run perfectly straight, could be hit from the side instead of astern.

Secondly, sometimes the wave ahead would be smaller than the original one. NIMBLE would go up the back and down over the front, picking up speed in a bewildering manner until she had done the same on three or four successive waves— giving the effect of a berserk roller coaster! There was apparently no danger, as we never could drive the bows under, but it was hard on the nerves.

Even more unnerving was the occasional comber which had a particularly steep face. NIMBLE would take off, apparently straight down in the vertical plane—headed for the abyss! This invariably scared the crew half to death, although there still was apparently no actual danger.

For these three reasons, then, we would reef down to a storm jib in lesser gales. NIMBLE would still surf, but more reluctantly, with adequate rudder control. No sail at all made her more sluggish, with waves bursting right at the transom.

CHAPTER 8

We experienced a period of ten days of continuous gales, and as we were apparently in a cyclonic situation, winds kept shifting all around.

This meant that seas would be coming from several directions at once—resulting in an unbelievable turbulence that none of us, regardless of our long sea-going experience, had ever encountered.

After a short while, it was inevitable not to think that it was impossible for any man-made structure to endure such an ordeal, as the boat was tossed, shaken, and jerked all at once. This continued for hour after hour, and for several days at a stretch—an interminable wrenching, accompanied by the unending shrieking of the wind—it would have been bad enough—but the noise of the wind, overpowering and pervading the entire atmosphere, seemed like the voice of doom, screaming in triumph over our pitiable minuteness and frailty in an endless seascape of twisted and tortured crashing seas.

Every once in a while the screaming did stop— to be replaced by an eerie brassy note—sounding like distant, muted trumpets.

"Surely," we thought, "now things are bound to get better—or worse."

What looks like a peaceful bit of sea is in reality a huge wave preparing to crest and break. On right is NIMBLE'S wake—made surfing down the face at 15 knots.

It made no difference to the strength of the wind nor the height of the waves, however, and after a short interval, the old howling was back with us.

One morning the Skipper awoke to feel the motion worse than ever—apparently the newest gale had somehow whipped itself into an even greater frenzy. But no—something was missing— the shrieking of the wind was gone!

He leaped out of his bunk to find the answer, to be met by an incredible sight. There was no wind at all, but the seas were jumbled in the wildest confusion, dashing aimlessly in every direction, often meeting one another and exploding skyward in a burst of spray. We were in the eye of the storm.

A few hours later a new gale arrived, from the NW as usual, and away we went again, complete with shrieking wind.

We had some rough days, but the nights were far worse. Shifting winds caused breaking seas which could not be seen in the darkness—after a while in such conditions the helmsman would flinch every time he heard the hiss of an approaching wave ready to break—it often would come at an angle, so the boat received the shock of white water from the side of the floats, shoving it several feet sideways in the sea.

The roughest rides in the lesser gales would occur when the boat would start to surf just as the wave upon which it was riding would break. The result was a fast slide down a distressingly bumpy surface, ending with a few wild bucks. These final gyrations were apparently inevitable in such a situation, and the man at the wheel had a good chance of being tossed bodily out of his chair.

Fortunately, such a performance was relatively rare, but particularly unwelcome in periods of lessened visibility.

In all this turmoil, the Skipper was anxiously searching for signs of strain, and although he appeared unconcerned to the crew, he after all, had designed and built this boat, and had the responsibility of three lives on his hands. He had constructed everything to be as strong as possible, consistent with his light-weight theories, but still had never considered punishment as brutal as this.

He would feel the joint where the cross-arms passed through the central hull, but there was never any sign of movement there. Most vulnerable was the float connective at the forward attachment of the pontoons, where the strain was most concentrated.

He would continuously but secretly study this point. Suddenly, after several days in the storms, he saw the floats moving ominously—and knew that any working here would soon result in disaster!

Out he went with a wrench, hoping against hope that the now loosened bolts would not turn inside the cross-arms when he tightened the nuts on the outside. Luckily, they did not, and so began a twice-daily inspection which continued until the bolts could be properly reached and finally tightened—on the beach at the Azores.

This necessary inspection pointed up the convenience of our ship-handling arrangements from the inside of the cabin. Let it storm all it wanted,

52 TRANS-ATLANTIC TRIMARAN

we were cozy and secure, although by this time everything below had become wet. The checking of the connectives had to be done on deck, however. As it was necessary to lie on the deck to reach the nuts on the under side of the cross-arms, waterproof clothing was no aid in keeping dry.

There was now no dry clothing to which to change after a visit outside, and it was most uncomfortable to come back below and sit around with one's garments streaming cold salt water.

And so the Skipper would make these trips while naked, and when returning to the cabin had the dubious satisfaction of donning things which were at least only well dampened. It seemed worthwhile to endure the stinging cold of the elements as long as he did not have to be completely soaked while below.

This would have made quite a picture—it could be captioned: "Man defies elements dressed only in Crescent wrench." He was clad in something more than just a wrench in these conditions, however, as he had a small life line around his waist.

The loosening of the bolts was a completely minor problem — except that it was difficult to fix at sea, unless inspection holes were chopped in the cross-arms so the bolt heads could be reached. This problem was later solved by using longer bolts. The portion beyond the nut was filed flat, so it could be held by a wrench or vice-grip tool while the adjacent nut was tightened.

As for the rest of the boat, not even the squeaks and groans normally associated with wooden craft ever appeared. This was due to the fact that glue is used on all mating surfaces, and the boat is literally one solid piece, with none of the wrench-

53 TRANS-ATLANTIC TRIMARAN

ing which would have occurred if we had had ballast.

In the midst of this stressful period, there occurred one of those illuminating episodes which can brighten the soul in moments of adversity.

Bill wanted to make a statement: "Skipper, regardless of what might happen, I want you to know that this has been a wonderful experience."

How can you answer such a declaration? It can only be done with the spirit, thanking all the Powers that such a man should exist, and doubly thankful that he was along as a shipmate.

The general direction in which we had been driven was SE, and after ten days of fleeing we found ourselves one thousand miles East of the United States, as well as several hundred miles South of our intended track—all done under jib alone. The jib was usually reefed down to storm proportions—imagine a thirty-foot boat going such a distance with only fifty square feet of sail! There was an encouraging note here, for if we ever had trouble with the mast, it would have been comparatively easy to set a jury rig which would be effective with but a small sail area.

Strangely enough, we would have been better off if we had had even more violent storms than we did, for in the major one we did encounter, we could surf across the larger waves, having more choice of direction. The subsequent gales had been less intense, being heavy enough so that we had to run before the seas, but which were not large enough to furnish us room to sail across.

Action of the breaking waves in these differing

conditions was interesting to watch, especially as we had long been addicted to the Hawaiian style of surf riding, and in consequence always made a study of these phenomena.

In the stronger gales the wave tops would topple forward, becoming definitely concave before breaking. In the lesser storms they would still break, but in a subsiding movement, which nevertheless was distinctly hazardous.

People have inquired as to NIMBLE's response in case we should meet the occasional gigantic comber which has wreaked havoc upon various yachts.

We have not yet encountered such a wave, but believe that the principle we have discovered in relation to NIMBLE's behavior in rugged conditions would still apply—the bigger the wave the less trouble we would have.

Our ten days of continuous gales had now ended —NIMBLE sat quietly upon a softly heaving sea— the peacefulness was a welcome relief after so much prolonged turbulence.

We would have welcomed the sun, for all our damp gear was now on deck in an effort to get rid of the moisture which had permeated every corner of our mobile domain.

The deck looked like the aftermath of an explosion in a clothing warehouse, but we were anxious to have things below dry once again.

If you have ever shoved reluctant bare feet deep into a soggy, cold sleeping bag you will appreciate our solicitude in this regard, for we usually slept rolled in a ball, making as little

55 TRANS-ATLANTIC TRIMARAN

contact as possible with our soaked bedding.

There was no wind, but we welcomed the respite, wishing only that the sun would appear. As a matter of fact, we practically never saw his cheerful countenance on the entire voyage. We were, of course, long overdue for a bath, but it was then just too cold for a plunge in frigid green depths surrounding us. We had promised ourselves plenty of swimming when we reached the meandering Gulf Stream, however.

We were in the region where we expected to encounter the prevailing SW wind, which was to waft us to England. And so we waited. Then waited some more—no wind.

We took stock of our food—it was disappearing at an alarming rate. We were supposed to have an adequate supply for forty days, but obviously someone had either underestimated the required amount or the capacity of three healthy men to consume same.

It was also evident that we were not going to make a fast passage, as any wind we did receive was always light and dead ahead. We wished for some means of communication with our families.

Also, a wire bridle arrangement which supported the stays was showing signs of wear, and we wished for some chain with which to replace it.

One bright spot was our store of water. We were using it at the rate of but one gallon per day for the entire ship, which was but two-thirds of our original estimate. We had water for sixty days.

In the light of our present necessities, then, we began studying our charts in order to determine where supplies and communications could be obtained. There was not much chance of our meeting a steamer, as we were now far from any shipping lanes, and had seen no vessels since our first day at sea.

There was no land anywhere near, but we noticed on the chart some tiny pin pricks 800 miles to the East. These were the Azores, and we knew they belonged to Portugal but that was all. Oddly enough, just before leaving the United States we had refused the offer of a chart showing these islands, as we had no intention of passing anywhere near them.

Without these local charts, we did not know which of these nine islands were even inhabited, but it looked as though we would have an opportunity of finding out. We were so far South by this time that these spots of earth were but a few hundred miles from our intended path to Plymouth.

And so we headed East with the same light and fickle winds, which we expected to become even more so, for the Azores lie in a permanent high-pressure area.

It took eight days to reach our next port, and it was easy to fall into the lazing routine which followed.

CHAPTER 9

Having a crew of three proved ideal. We had watches of three hours on and six hours off. This interval meant that one's duty occurred at a different time each day.

With so much free time, we seemed to be always just lying around, chatting or brewing goodies; and napping whenever we felt so inclined. It was a most restful arrangement, especially as NIMBLE was often steering herself, so that the helmsman had little to do. Our voyage was probably the most comfortable one yet taken in a small craft, due to the qualities of our unique vessel.

Our many discussions embraced practically every subject known to man, with a surprisingly small proportion being expended upon that ubiquitous subject—women.

The Skipper said, in some surprise, "Here I am a good deal older than you fellows, and yet I seem to be the only one aboard with a healthy interest in girls!"

George said he could take 'em or leave 'em alone, and as Bill had been married a short while, he had but a single though intense focus concerning this subject. Although he said little, the fact that he had his hair cut twice during our subsequent five-day stay at the Azores gave him away.

Once, when George happened to be asleep, Bill and the Skipper did get into quite a discussion in this domain.

Here were two similar men, both imaginative and adventurous. What sort of wife would appeal to this type?

"From my experience," said the Skipper, "the most important factor is simple faith on the part of the wife. It is hard enough to battle the whole world without having to fight your wife, too. One little word of encouragement can do wonders for the morale. Yes, I would say that to have her believe in him is easily the most desired quality such a man would want in his spouse."

"As I understand it," said Bill, "it requires a good deal of moral courage to believe in someone, for you can't have faith in someone else if you don't first have faith in yourself. Does this mean that women in general must have more character than men?"

"I believe that it does, and although it may not be fair to expect women to have more of that rarest of qualities, moral courage, than men, that is the way it is. Besides, Nature intended woman to complement man—not to compete with him. I also believe that woman cannot completely fulfill herself unless she is truly devoted to her man. Modern woman, at least American woman, refuses to accept this fact because she feels it makes her subservient and dilutes her status as an individual."

"In other words, then, by denying her own nature, woman is foredoomed to discontent?"

"Yes, for man must do what he must do, and his woman backs him up."

George grins from the helmsman's hatch while Bill (with Sextant) waits for the sun to appear through clouds (as usual).

World War II experiences were revived, although Bill's had consisted of being rejected by various Service branches because he was a half-inch over the six-foot-six height maximum.

The Skipper had spent four years in Arizona as a flying instructor, teaching fighter gunnery. "It was great," he said, "the most flying fun imaginable. Just like the movies—you would take a bead on the flying target, pull the trigger, rat-a-tat-tat, and then break away by turning the aircraft almost upside down. It was also rewarding, for we worked out a technique at our school which resulted in unprecedented scores." He also grew fond of the desert country. "You could awaken every morning and know for certain that the sun would shine that very day."

George had become so enamored of the Orient that he had returned there after being discharged from the Army. His career was varied—everything from inventing and marketing an electric water heater, owning a night club, to teaching English in a Japanese university.

Bill and George were highly educated and widely traveled, and opened to the Skipper a new world of philosophy and general knowledge. If an obscure mathematical formula was required for some current problem, for instance, one of these two would just dredge it out of their memory, and apply it. It certainly was a handy accomplishment. They had both also read all of any books which apparently mattered, and would for hours discuss minute details of the various viewpoints of the authors and assorted characters.

The Skipper had never considered himself as any sort of an intellectual, although of the two branches of the intellect, knowledge and creative thinking, he had some acquaintance with the latter. The knowledge part obviously did not belong to him—at least general knowledge, although he did remember quite a few facts about boating.

This seemed to be his field, for he found himself fulfilled with his designing and experimenting. "Man is happiest when he is creating something," he said, "and if that something is beautiful, useful, provides healthful recreation, and is profitable as well, he can ask for little more."

The reluctance of sailors in general to accept these new boats also came under discussion. Of course, in any striving for new human experience there are traditional obstacles of inertia, vested interest, and power—to say nothing of fear of the unknown. You can't reason with fear. Most sailors seem to want boats to stay exactly the same as they have been for centuries, and want no improvements if the boats have to be different.

Several times as the Skipper had sailed past yacht clubs he had the experience of seeing men run out on the dock, waving their fists in rage and bellowing, "Get that horrible (or words to that effect) thing out of here!" These worthies doubtless had their inhibitions modified by a visit to the club bar, but the sentiments were unmistakable.

However, this attitude is now changing with the appearance of the multihull in larger numbers upon the yachting scene. The small racing catamaran is playing a large part in this familiarization. It obviously completely outclasses the traditional dinghy it is replacing, and we believe that the trimaran holds the identical position with regard to cruising sailboats.

So much for what we call the "brass-bound" sailor. As for our participation in the discoveries of the solutions which overcame various traditional difficulties of the multihulled boat, we have found it a fascinating and rewarding search. The apparent typical solution is largely based upon attitude—if you could be completely objective and unprejudiced (meaning unafraid) concerning any facet of design and of the sea, the problems seemed to solve themselves.

Perhaps our basic outlook is just different from other mariners, for we seem to be more surf-riders than sailors, for to us the ocean is just a great big playground, and the bigger the waves the more fun it is.

Our boats are merely the instruments of liaison between us and the sea, and as they seem as indestructible as our surf boards, they appear to be merely the extension of the smaller units.

The traditional sailor is not necessarily afraid of the sea, but has learned to respect it to such a degree that he might as well fear it, in the relation between his boat and the manner in which it must be handled, for it is not only expensive but is comparatively easily damaged.

Some people love the sea for itself. It can be dangerous, of course, but it can also be dared and challenged—for the important fact is that man always has a chance with the sea, and in actions and situations which seem suicidal to the average sailor, this individual is merely enjoying himself.

A reflection of this attitude occurred several years ago, when the Skipper and his friend Fred had spent a few hair-raising hours defying the roughest water of which boisterous San Francisco

63 TRANS-ATLANTIC TRIMARAN

Bay is capable. They were in one of his dinghies —which incidentally differ from other dinghies almost as much as his multihulls differ from conventional boats.

They had worked out a system of jibing in strong winds, and indeed, would go tearing downwind in 40-knot gusts, deliberately jibing repeatedly—a sight which is simply unbelievable, for this maneuver is the most dangerous which can be effected in ordinary craft in strong winds.

The two sailors were on the way home when the Skipper said, "Do you know what we are?" His companion looked at him questioningly. "We're just a couple of big kids in an overgrown toy."

This seems to be our attitude. Our boats are so inexpensive we do not have the usual financial responsibility, and they are so seaworthy that they are seemingly immune to the ravages of the sea, although of course some skill is required in extreme conditions.

One secret of jibing the dinghy is, of course, related to light weight, for the aluminum boom of this sixteen-foot craft weighed only three pounds, and apparently could hit against the shrouds with any amount of force without causing damage. The rest of the secret consists of holding the boom down as it swings across the center line, and turning the boat so when the boom does hit the stays, the craft is turning in the opposite direction from that used when starting the maneuver. Thus the usual centrifugal forces which intensify the jibe are counteracted, and the boom hitting the stays merely gives the light boat a push ahead, with no apparent turning moment.

You might be interested in hearing about the first time our dinghy jibing technique received the acid test, even though it had been previously worked out in theory.

We were in Raccoon Straits near San Francisco, and a violent squall was pushing us onto a sheer, rocky headland. The wind was so strong that the steeply-heeled boat would not go into it, but instead was being shoved sideways. Because we were not going ahead, with no water passing by the rudder, we could not come about.

We waited anxiously for the wind to lighten so we could claw off the land, but it kept pushing us closer and closer. The Skipper sang out: "Stand by to jibe!"

It looked certain that we would end up a splintered wreck on that forbidding cliff as we turned and rushed directly at it with terrifying speed, but the bow swung around with only a few precious inches to spare and away we went, reaching out of danger. After that, we knew there was practically no situation which could not be mastered by our little craft.

How is it jibing one of our multihulls? Here is one of the biggest surprises for the conventional sailor, and is but another reason why our boats make him uncomfortable—apparent witchcraft!

We entertain ourselves by jibing these boats in strong winds—just to watch the reactions of our sailor guests. It is uncanny when compared with other types, at that. The boom will swing rapidly, although of course our greater speed through the water minimizes it in relation to our forward movement. In any event, as the boom swings across to the end of the mainsheet—the boat does not even heel! There is merely a "click" as the sheets snap out to full length. Great stability keeps the craft upright.

Of course, when we are not deliberately showing off, we jibe in heavy weather by pulling the boom to amidships, and slacking it out rapidly as the ship jibes. In a conventional boat, an accidental jibe in heavy weather is an invitation to almost certain disaster to some portion of the rig.

CHAPTER 10

In our search for a more seaworthy craft, as well as an inexpensive one, we must admit to an evangelistic fervor.

The idea is this: In a world of constantly-increasing restriction and regimentation, the independent individual faces a greater and greater confinement in every dimension. It seems to us that soon the only refuge will be the sea, and here such a man can, for a time at least, have a chance to be his own master.

Because of the ease of operating NIMBLE from the pilot's post, it was practically never necessary to disturb the off-watch. Even if it was required in a squall, the relief man would merely steady the wheel while the man on watch would be projected out of the hatch, reefing the sails.

It is traditional in small boats that the crew gets a tremendous amount of exercise, mostly from just hanging on while he laboriously tries to change his position as the craft rolls, pitches, and jumps. We found it just the opposite in NIMBLE, and in fact the lack of exercise proved almost a booby-trap later on.

When we did subsequently reach port, we discovered that our legs were as weak as if we had

George in mid-ocean test of life line

spent the previous period in bed, and indeed, were quite bothered with cramps of the upper legs while climbing to our third-story hotel rooms, or tramping about the hilly Azorean countryside.

Having heard how sailors had difficulty in walking upon reaching shore after having been at sea, George had it all figured out—"As soon as we land, I'm going to CRAWL to the nearest lamp post, pull myself up, and then go from there."

This proved unnecessary, as we felt no discomfort in the transition from our steady boat to stone-still land.

The lack of exercise, however, as evidenced by our unwilling legs, is not to be ignored, especially for anyone who plans to do any walking after going ashore on a cruise. On our subsequent sail to England, we all practiced a routine of calisthenics, and had no further difficulty while ashore. It was rather comical, as we each had our favorite exercises, the most important of which was the knee bend. Bill was a great knee-bender, while George liked to jump up and down on the fore deck. The Skipper observed this last with some misgivings, as the three-eights-inch decking, which although sufficiently strong, would still deflect an appreciable distance when the feet would land on a spot between the framing.

Our cooking facilities consisted of one small gimballed stove, which boasted but a single burner of the Primus type, and which unfortunately was of the smallest size. It was cute, and used practically no fuel, but took an appreciable time to boil water, so there was a lot of waiting around for food, although this of course just added to the pleasure when it finally did arrive.

It is hard to describe just how good victuals are when at sea. The clean, pure air just seems to do something to the taste buds, for ordinary flavors appear magnified, and even the smallest bits of spice fairly burst into miniature explosions of pure pungency.

Bill was the cook, and George the dish-washer as well as navigator. Because the little stove burned kerosene, the bottom of our single pot and frying pan soon became caked with soot, and were so difficult to scour that we soon tired of the attempt, always taking care to place them on a single section of our galley work table, so as to confine the dirty area. Our next stove will be of the alcohol variety, which is clean, even though the odor which accompanies this type is slightly sickening. However, the olfactory senses are apparently the most adaptable, and perhaps this would soon become unnoticed. We would use a larger burner for more heat.

Bill and George were both epicures, and it was interesting to see how such limited cooking facilities as were ours could turn out uniformly delicious meals.

We had but one burner, of course, and only one pot, and it took so long to boil water that it would have been impracticable to have multi-course meals. So, we had the one-pot variety, and they form one of the pleasantest memories of the entire journey.

Here is a typical day's menu. For breakfast we would have tinned fruit juice, oatmeal, scrambled eggs with bacon, coffee, and a sandwich if desired.

70 TRANS-ATLANTIC TRIMARAN

We had no facilities for making toast, and it was not missed. The cereal would be made by adding powdered milk to the water, and so it would come out already creamy, so that no milk was necessary on top of it. A generous helping of granulated sugar would be placed in the bottom of the bowl, and each man would stir this mixture industriously—how good it tasted!

For lunch we would invariably have soup — always of the dried variety, and it was invariably great. We used mostly the ones made by a great tea manufacturer, but had also discovered that some made by a Swiss concern were delicious, indeed. We ate innumerable sandwiches at this time. Bill was the champion sandwich consumer. A typical concoction would contain, besides the usual two slices of bread—generous slices of raw onion, pickle relish, a huge slab of cheese, and jam. He had a difficult time restricting this production to wide-open-mouth size.

We had some fun with peanut butter. When first discussing what foods to take, George had suggested peanut butter. He had not had any for some years, but thought it might be welcome. He was immediately voted down by Bill and the Skipper, who remembered it as some sticky stuff which just glues one's teeth together.

Anyway, a single jar was taken along for George. You are right—he got little of it, as the others suddenly decided it was wonderful when lubricated with jam.

"When we get to the Azores," said George, "I'm going to lay in a one-gallon supply of peanut butter, and then I'm going to hide it from you bandits." Sad to say, the Azoreans had never even heard of it, and the same goes for the English. Assumedly, George has gone on a straight peanut butter diet since his return home.

He objected to the use of marmalade on the trip. It seemed that our folding chart table was too much trouble to set up, so George did all his navigating on a little table in the galley. When our countless sandwiches were made, there usually were some charts already on this table, so they became well covered with the ingredients.

"Darn it, fellows, watch out with that marmalade," George warned, "any other jam is OK, but marmalade is so slippery I can't write through it when plotting our position on the chart."

Our main meal would come at the end of the day, and was eagerly looked forward to. It would almost invariably begin with a salad made of shredded cabbage, raw. This vegetable kept well, and we were lucky to have enough of it, as we became veritable addicts. Bill would make a dressing, of which the main ingredients would be mayonnaise and tomato ketchup. To this was added mustard and various spices. He would always announce in regard to the salad, "Dressing's on the bottom." We did not ask why it was never on the top, but perhaps stirring it around so that it covered the cabbage helped heighten our anticipation.

Our one-pot main course would usually approximate the following: first in the pot would go a generous portion of sliced onions, sauteed in margarine. We took this spread in preference to butter because it apparently lasts indefinitely without refrigeration—which we did not have. Base of the dish was Bulgar grain; the kind used in making

Pilaf. A can of luncheon meat of the ham variety would be added after being chopped in small pieces. A can of vegetables, a packet of soup or a bouillon cube, plus various spices, would result in a dish which was marvelous to encounter. A whole pot full would give each of us two great bowls-full. The meal would be topped off with coffee and bar chocolate, or perhaps some more sandwiches. Bread and jam is the sailor's dessert. The cereal base of the meal would be alternated with pasta.

Apparently the main ingredients for successful cookery as we practiced it are onions and tomato sauce—we had a plentiful supply of each.

Just which foods to take on such a trip are always a problem, even if expertly-compiled lists are available.

We felt that we could not have eaten any better, especially in regard to our meager cooking facilities.

We found that dark bread will keep indefinitely if well wrapped in aluminum foil. Eggs which are fresh in the market sense will not do but eggs fresh in the producer's sense are something else again—we took along a three weeks' supply, and they did not spoil. We had heard of various ways of storing eggs, some of them messy, such as being dipped in lard and packed in sawdust; some of them troublesome, such as turning them every day. However, just plain fresh eggs worked well in our case.

We had a flitch of bacon, and a large amount of cheese. It all kept well. We did have a little spoilage of packaged cereal, but that was because of careless stowage, which allowed some water to get upon it.

73 TRANS-ATLANTIC TRIMARAN

We also tried cooking with salt water, but gave it up as a bad job after testing the results, cooked with varying ratios of salt to fresh water. Apparently, sea water has a large proportion of chemicals in addition to plain salt—in any event, the food we cooked in it was not good.

Because we had built and fitted a boat at so modest a figure, we thought it apropos to experiment with a low cost diet, which would be a logical development. We discounted fishing, partly from stories we had read of the scarcity of these creatures at times when they were most needed, and partly because the Skipper is too kind hearted to kill anything.

Our projected low-budget diet was to be based upon wheat, and we had been instructed by our Hungarian friend, Tony, how to prepare this after grinding it in a small mill which was supposed to be readily available in hardware stores.

It was estimated that we could thus live on but thirty cents per man per day, and should buy our wheat at some feed stores. It seemed that the grade sold for chicken feed was the best value, for although its appearance was not uniform, it was just as nutritive, and at a lower price.

The only hitch to this plan was the fact that we failed to find such a mill, and as the day of departure threatened, we abandoned the project. It was later discovered that a coffee grinder would have sufficed.

All this time we were approaching the Azores. The weather was light, with shifting winds, and it was overcast, as usual. We had only two opportunities to swim on the entire voyage, although later Bill did take a dip in the English Channel. The water there was so cold we thought we could see his feet turn blue before they disappeared from sight as he dove.

We would have liked to be able to swim frequently, but it was just too cold. When we did see the sun it was just for a little while at a time, and as it was invariably overcast at dawn and dusk, we never had an opportunity of taking star sights.

There were many porpoises about, however, and they were always a joy. We did no fishing, although we did have a surplus survival fishing kit.

Our life line dragged astern. It had several knots at the end, and was the source of curiosity for countless sea birds. Apparently its movement through the water gave a very fish-like effect.

One of these birds obviously fell in love with NIMBLE. Never had he seen so stately and graceful a creature as was our ship—with spreading wings of dazzling whiteness and effortless, purposeful passage. He followed us for hundreds of miles, and we looked for him daily. We could sympathize with him in unrequited love, however, knowing that he, like some wingless birds we knew, could stand such aloofness for only so long. He finally disappeared, and some wag aboard (we had three of them) remarked that he had gone to seek a more responsive mate — for everyone knows that one good Tern deserves another!

When five hundred miles from the Azores, we encountered a turtle which was about two feet wide across his shell. He was floating under a short log, and which obviously had been in the

We speak our first ship. Bill waves while the Skipper photographs French merchantman.

water a long time. We could not imagine what a turtle would be doing so far from land—if it had been a lady turtle, and she had wanted to lay some eggs on a beach—she would have had a mighty long swim.

We had seen several ships from a distance, and shortly before reaching the Azores spoke our first one. It was a French freighter, and she changed course to cross our stern at a distance of only several feet.

Bill and George both speak French, and there was a spirited exchange as she swept by, with her master handling her as surely as he would a small runabout.

Naturally we were anxious to learn our position, and of course wanted to check the accuracy of George's vaunted wrist watch. The time was checked, and George was jubilant when his time piece was right on the button! Jubilation turned to dismay, however, when, as the steamer lengthened her distance, the watch proved to be one hour slow!

This was a bitter blow, and what had been complacency a few moments earlier turned to bewilderment and a helpless feeling. The ocean suddenly seemed vastly larger and emptier than it had previously appeared.

Then ensued a council of war. The situation was discussed and analyzed, with no apparent solution until Bill had a thought. "Suppose the French use a meridian other than Greenwich?" Then came a frantic search through our various navigational publications. Sure enough — the French use the time at the Paris Observatory, which is just one hour earlier than Greenwich.

TRANS-ATLANTIC TRIMARAN

George was vindicated. His watch was henceforth regarded with awe and affection.

The next test was not of the timepiece, however, but of the navigator himself, for according to calculations, we would early the next morning pass forty-five miles South of the Island of Flores, which is one of the two most Northerly of the Group. If we were lucky, we should be able to see the loom of the lighthouse.

CHAPTER 11

George had the pre-dawn watch, and had been straining his eyes Northward for hours. This was the crucial test for him! He could hardly wait for the Skipper to replace him as pilot, so that he could proudly point out a very faint but quite distinct flash of light above the far horizon.

That was George's first landfall, and as far as the rest of the crew was concerned, made him the World's foremost navigator. This appreciation was further heightened by our final landing at England.

We later learned that the Island of Flores is largely agricultural, as are the rest of these Islands. The most Westerly and most remote of them, it is, as its name indicates, noted for its flowers. The capital is Santa Cruz, and is remarkable for huge masses of hydrangeas.

It has a tiny neighbor, named Corvo, which is the smallest of the Azores. It is an extinct volcano, eight miles in circumference. There is but one tiny village, and the inhabitants tend herds of a special breed of miniature cattle, which are pale coffee-colored. The summit of this Island is topped with a secondary crater, containing a lake with a number of tiny islets.

The following day we could expect to see the Island of Pico, which is seven thousand feet in elevation. It lay directly beyond our goal, Fayal. Whether or not either were inhabited was a different question altogether, but we were sure that one of the several adjacent islands would contain people.

One situation intrigued us. Our light list showed that the lighthouse on the near end of Fayal was no longer in operation. This seemed strange, for you might think that lighthouses should multiply as time goes by, rather than diminish. However, this question was resolved after we had landed, and learned something about these fascinating bits of earth.

We had seen many whales at this period, mostly looking like great, dark reefs upon which the water sullenly swirled.

That evening, however, we sailed right through a group of them, and it was disconcerting to see these tremendous creatures upon every hand, for our boat would have become but a bunch of kindling if they had become playful.

These whales presented a most curious appearance as some of them raised their heads in the water. They possessed amazingly thin lower jaws, which were knotted with rough lumps. They looked somewhat like a small boat which is down by the head, the transom sticking up out of the water, and with the top section of an unbelievably bumpy mast exposed to view. We learned later that these were sperm whales.

We had heard that the Azoreans were famed for their primitive method of whaling, with man being pitted against beast in the traditional manner, with no modern methods of whaling being available to them. We could tell them where the whales were, all right!

In the meantime, our bits of stationary cloud did indeed reveal solid land below, and we sailed for hours with Pico in view. We could expect to reach Fayal on the following morning.

In order to appear more presentable we cleaned up the ship, with Bill going so far as to shave off several weeks of beard. The Skipper had been shaving every day with a small electric unit with self-contained batteries. It was not very efficient compared with the shaver powered by home electricity, but did its job, nevertheless. The batteries lasted several months. George had developed a luxurious crop of shiny black whiskers, and looked so distinguished he preferred to retain them.

The next morning at dawn found us coasting along the shores of Fayal. It was inhabited, all right, for we could see a continuous line of houses, flanking a road along the hilly shore. Every several houses seemed to justify a church, with all being constructed of stone, with tile roofs. The land was obviously intensively cultivated.

We rounded one point and then another, being certain that the road we saw must inevitably lead to some kind of port. We were hoping that we would not have to circumnavigate the entire island before finding this spot. We were also on the lookout for fishermen who might direct us. We did see several small row boats, but they were always too far distant to hail.

We rounded a low point—and there we were! A handsome breakwater met our gaze, and already a pilot boat had put to sea to meet us. It was thrilling.

81 TRANS-ATLANTIC TRIMARAN

The motor craft approached, containing a half-dozen men in uniform who regarded us with great curiosity. No one spoke, apparently waiting for the other group to put forth first feelers as might regard a language difficulty.

Then, too, we were not too certain of our status, for we had not planned to visit these parts, and were not certain of a reception without any official preparations. We were wondering how we could ask asylum as distressed mariners when our vessel was in good condition.

Our flag was flying, however, so at least our origin was obvious. The man in charge of the pilot boat finally spoke. He did know some English, and although we had to ask him to repeat a number of phrases, we had little difficulty on that score.

They passed us a line, and with our sails furled, we had an opportunity of looking about us. The town of Horta was a pleasant surprise, looking like a Mediterranean village with rows of stone houses, painted in pastel colors. Churches were much in evidence, usually constructed in distinctive black and white. The place was extensive, containing as it does a population of ten thousand—half the population of the Island.

CHAPTER 12

We were soon tied to the stone quay, where a surprisingly large crowd had gathered, considering the earliness of the hour. This crowd was to remain large and nearly always present for the remainder of our stay. The Portuguese are of course great sailors, and we often wondered what they actually thought of our boat. We tried to follow their remarks concerning it, but were never sure of the gist of them.

We were informed that we must await the arrival of the Port Doctor. This worthy arrived in a few minutes, and he, too, spoke a little English. He solemnly scanned our Bill of Health, and appeared satisfied. There were no other formalities except filling out a paper describing our boat —its size, method of propulsion, capacity. That ended the official part of the reception, although we were asked to later visit the Port Captain. Our passports were never mentioned.

Horta is undisturbed by travelers, and this isolation is reflected in a people so friendly that it is most refreshing. Our first taste of this attitude came when we went to a nearby quayside bath house, where showers were somewhat more than welcome. When the attendant learned we were strangers, he went to his little vegetable plot and presented each of us with a head of lettuce. It was

NIMBLE at quayside, Horta, Azores.

quite touching, even though we could not understand the other's language.

The first word we did learn, however, was "Thank you,"—an expression we were to use innumerable times during our stay.

Learning that NIMBLE would be safe when left alone, we decided to enjoy life, and spend the next day or so at a hotel. An accommodating chap named Jose, who with his father operated the Cafe Sport close by, offered to guide us to the inn. On the way we stopped at his place of business, where we saw evidence of the passage of many well-known yachts and yachtsmen. We determined to send back a photograph of our boat after our return home. We later did.

The walk up the long, narrow main street was intriguing. A gang of men was working on the cobbled pavement, and were hammering new stones in place with great wooden tampers, looking like inverted wooden buckets at the end of handles several feet long. "Not much like the United States, eh?" inquired our guide.

It was not, and we were glad. There were innumerable tiny shops along the street, and few seemed to be devoted to any particular type of merchandise. Most of them carried odd bits of apparently unrelated articles, as if they had ordered them from a mail order concern with an odd catalogue containing only numbers—no pictures or descriptions.

A few small taxis were in evidence, and indeed, their drivers were the only people we met who seemed to have any feeling for the old familiar push for business. They were still different from the type driver to which we had become accustomed, for when you shook your head with a smile, using two fingers to indicate you preferred to walk, they would either smile or laugh, and resume their lounging against their machines.

The sidewalks were barely of sufficient width to accommodate two people, so many walked in the street. This was of little concern, however, as automobile traffic was sparse. There were, however, a goodly number of motorized bicycles.

The sidewalks were of dark stones, inlaid with white ones in a variety of patterns and shapes. A new terrace was being constructed in a small park by the water, and it was interesting to watch how the artisans inlaid the stones. The city was obviously old, as the inlaid white stones were considerably less worn than their darker fellows, and in many places stood considerably higher than the latter.

There were two hotels in town, and as the first one appeared almost minuscule in size, we walked to the most pretentious one, which was right in the middle of the city.

We were lucky we had a guide, for there was no sign on the outside of the three story building, and after we went in we could not even find an office.

Finally the manager was located, and then ensued a torrent of Portuguese, while we waited to learn from our interpreter what all this was going to cost.

It was decided that we would each be charged the equivalent of $2.15 per day. This did not sound too bad, but after we learned that this price also included three delicious multi-course meals, we knew we had something!

Of course, there were a few drawbacks, which did not bother us. The plumbing did not always work, and a bath cost extra (twelve cents). The shower was precious. It consisted of a bucket, to be filled and then hoisted on a rope, with a spigot on the bottom.

Biggest surprise came when we retired for the night. The Skipper moved in bed, and was astonished to hear a rustling noise. He investigated. Sure enough—the mattress was made of straw! Here was something—he had never expected to actually sleep on what sailors used to call a "donkey's breakfast."

In the morning he watched the maid make the bed. The top of the mattress cover contained four long slits, through which her hands could rearrange the straw.

"Here is an improvement over the modern mattress," he thought, "custom adjustment to fit anatomical peculiarities!"

Our life at Horta could not have been more restful. There was not a bit of night life, except for a few people sitting around in coffee houses, and the cinema. Current attraction at the movies was an antique affair purportedly filmed in India by American movie makers; which we estimated to be about twenty-five years old.

Street lights went out about nine o'clock, when two of the four diesel generators serving the city were turned off. The same applied to the hotel corridors, and we would go through long passages and up three flights of stairs in pitch blackness. All seemed perfectly safe, however, as apparently crime is unknown here. Lone women could be seen making their way down darkened streets with no evident apprehension.

We had expected to stay at Horta only a day or so, but as a strong NE wind arose, which would have been right in our teeth, we waited five days, until it blew itself out.

The delay was actually welcomed, as all the Azoreans just knocked themselves out to do all they could for us, with no thought of the time involved, and with no regard for personal gain.

Actual working time on NIMBLE took only about an hour, and our faithful craft appeared lonely though eager as she sat by the quay. Customs guard patrolled the area, and we were not worried as to her safety.

The rest of the interval was spent in sightseeing and visiting with our many newly-found friends, and we were so entranced by the entire picture that we delved into the history of this fascinating area.

CHAPTER 13

There are many marks of antiquity about the Azores, but this is not too surprising, as they were first settled in 1441. They must have been known long before that time, but apparently no one got around to actual colonization until Portugal first colonized San Miguel, which is the largest of the chain of nine islands. It is about forty miles in length, by nine miles. Ponta Delgada is the name of the capital city there.

This is a very fertile island, and the damp Atlantic climate and constant sea mists contribute to the ease of pastoral living.

All of the islands are of volcanic origin, and this subterranean activity still persists in various localities.

This is the reason why the lighthouse on Fayal which we had hoped to see while approaching the Azores was no longer in use. It seems that this structure is now one-half mile inland, and the eruption which formed new land to seaward of it occurred as recently as 1957.

This is perhaps another reason why Americans are received in so friendly a manner there—at the time of these eruptions the United States were most generous with aid, and the resulting gratitude of the natives both for material help and easing of immigration arrangements has helped in the establishment of friendly relations.

89 TRANS-ATLANTIC TRIMARAN

There has been extensive migration to the United States from the Azores.

A number of people asked us if we had heard of a California town named Sausalito. Had we! This is but a few miles from the Skipper's home at Mill Valley, and he had actually lived in Sausalito for several years prior to World War II. NIMBLE had been moored there preceding our departure for the Atlantic.

It seemed that the family of a well-known Sausalito boat builder originated at the Island of Pico, close to Fayal, so the name of the American town was a familiar one. There was great surprise when it was learned the Skipper actually knew some members of the emigrated family. Small world.

A similar geographic coincidence obtained in relation to our official point of departure in the United States, which was Fall River, Massachusetts.

We were asked several times where we had left home, and we would answer, "Fall River, Massachusetts." We would emphasize the word "Massachusetts," hoping our listeners might at least have heard of the State—we were certain they had never heard of such a small town as Fall River.

To our surprise, however, they invariably appeared pleased, and would say, "Oh yes, Fall River." It seems that in regard to extensive migrations to the United States, we discovered that more Azoreans had moved to Fall River than perhaps any other American City!

The winter weather there must have appeared pretty grim to the emigrants, for although the

Azores are usually misty, the climate as a whole is moderate.

Our neighboring island was of course Pico, which is the most mountainous of them all. It still smokes from time to time, and we had become well acquainted with its towering appearance as we approached Fayal, where we had hoped to find some sort of a port. Some port! Horta is one of the finest on the whole Atlantic.

We did not get a chance to visit Pico, but were told that it was not nearly so cosmopolitan and wordly as was Fayal. Pico has apparently very little soil, with lava dominating the landscape. However, it is noted for wines, and there must be some soil in which to grow grapes. We took a gallon each of red and white Pico wine when we left for England. We were told that the white wine would not "travel" but perhaps before our arrival the wine did not have an opportunity of traveling on so sea-kindly a vessel as is ours. At any rate, the white wine seemed as good as ever upon our reaching Plymouth.

The second island of importance, after San Miguel, is Terceira, where an America air base is located, and where the musically-inclined Azoreans go to perform at the night clubs.

Most Easterly of the islands is Santa Maria, and this is the site of the large Air Terminal where a number of trans-Atlantic planes land. The travelers who pass through apparently consider the Azores as just a handy airplane filling station, as few stay over to visit these lands of long ago which are here now.

Of all the islands, the name we preferred was Graciosa, and although we did not see this smaller place, it is said to be one of the least mountainous, with a number of pretty villages, and picturesque lakes.

The Island of San Jorge is close to Fayal and Pico, and we had the opportunity of studying its strongly-ridged backbone of a prominent mountain range as we sailed by. It is said to be sparsely populated, and if anyone likes solitude, we can tell him where to find it. Even in comparatively crowded Fayal, a cottage may be rented for as little as $8 per month.

The only island we actually visited was Fayal, but we did get quite well acquainted with it in our five-day stay.

It is mostly farming land, but the many elaborate villas which lie on the hills above the town must be the result of income other than that from the many small rock-fenced farms, largely managed by peasant proprietors.

There is some industry—several whaling stations and a tuna cannery.

There seemed to be quite a bit of work on the roads and pavement, and this was apparently the result of made work to aid farmers who lost their means of livelihood following the 1957 earthquake, during which lava and ash covered quite a bit of land at the Western end of the Island. This eruption was the same one which moved the former lighthouse a half mile inland.

The Azorean physique is apparently average as we consider it, and very tall people are seemingly unkown here. Bill's six-foot-six-inch height was a sensation. Children would stop and gape at him open-mouthed. The adults were more restrained, however, and would wait until he had passed, and then would stop and turn around for a good look.

George was also somewhat of a curiosity, for whiskers were also a novelty, and our navigator looked distinguished, indeed. We thought it would be easy to sell a portrait of him to either the people who had made his trusty wrist watch, or to some sextant manufacturer, posed with their product. We had not actually gotten around to taking such studies, however, when George shaved off his hirsute glory before reaching Plymouth.

The Skipper felt completely inconspicuous in the presence of his outstanding companions, and was sure that few people even noticed him.

Strangely enough, Horta is the world's largest cable center, with some fourteen cables from all nations converging at this point. During World War II there was feverish activity in this industry, with some three hundred non-Azoreans engaged in it.

At the time of our visit this number had dwindled to about thirty such persons, and many empty residences surrounded the cable complex. End of the war was one reason for the lessened activity, the training of Azoreans to perform many of the jobs was another, but the most important, however, was the fact that the invention of modern equipment had made most of the work automatic in nature.

We met a number of the cable people, and were received by them in a friendly manner. Bill and the Skipper had occasion to visit the manager of the largest American company, who lived well up on the hill overlooking Horta, with a beautiful vista

NIMBLE on the beach at Horta.

of green land, blue sea, and the Island of Pico looming in the distance.

Our host interpreted the remarks of the Azorean maid who had admitted us to the residence. She announced us with the remark, "There are two men at the door, but one of them is so tall that I was afraid to let him in the house!"

During the long ensuing conversation the cable manager expressed his liking for the natives, but described them as "primitive." This brought an immediate denial from his wife, who wanted to compare some of the Azorean customs with the heraldic ones of his native country, England. We thought she had a good point there.

The name of the street on which the cable people lived had an intriguing name—it was Rua Consul Dabney. This name did not sound very Portuguese, and we were surprised to learn that it was an American name, and that it had a significant connection with the development of the Islands.

The original Dabney was John Bass Dabney, a Bostonian who had first visited the Islands in 1795 on a voyage during which he was seeking news of a relative who was drowned near Fayal.

He became interested in the area, and returned there in 1804 as United States Consul. He instituted various commercial enterprises, most of which were apparently successful.

He established a dynasty, his son and grandson also becoming United States Consul after him. The Dabney name was prominent in the area for nearly ninety years—by the end of that time there were none left bearing the historic name.

We spent some time conversing with the head

95 TRANS-ATLANTIC TRIMARAN

pilot for the Port of Horta, who had a fascinating collection of memorata of the various yachts which had called there. He had letters from many of the voyagers, as well as pictures of their boats. It was interesting to see this material, concerning as it did familiar names and vessels.

CHAPTER 14

We had seen the Port Doctor several times during our stay at Horga, and it was obvious we would have no trouble in obtaining from him the Bill of Health we would need as part of our entrance formalities in England.

It was quite a surprise, therefore, when we finally asked him for this document, we were firmly refused! He stated that such a paper was obsolete because of modern communications, and if the authorities in England wanted to know whether or not there was pestilence in Horta, they could telegraph and find out for themselves!

And so, the remainder of the journey contained a moral hazard, and we could picture ourselves marooned in quarantine for forty days while the rest of the Slocum racers disappeared over the horizon in the direction of victory.

Reprovisioning of our vessel in the Azores presented a somewhat more complicated task than at the supermarket back in America.

We had investigated various foods obtainable there, and were glad to discover that tuna was canned on the Island, and was quite inexpensive. Bananas were plentiful, being grown there as well. They were a much smaller variety than we had been accustomed to at home, and appeared green even when ripe. The flavor was good, however.

97 TRANS-ATLANTIC TRIMARAN

One luxury purchase we could not resist, and that consisted of two fresh pineapples, which were grown under glass on one of the neighboring islands. They cost about one dollar each, which was pure extravagance, in light of our vanishing exchequer, but the subsequent sampling of these delicious tropical tid-bits out on the broad Atlantic was a high-light of the trip.

Bread was a problem, as there was no flour obtainable except the white variety, although this did come in two grades. We had desired dark bread because of its superior keeping qualities. This was unknown here.

And so, we had the bread baked in loaves, rather than in the roll shape which was locally prevalent. It was double-baked, as we had heard that this procedure made bread keep longer. It kept for the remainder of the voyage, all right, and in addition provided dandy exercise for our teeth and jaws. That bread was the consistency of tire-tread, and although the flavor was good, eating it took some determination.

Bananas and cabbage were bought in one of the little vegetable stands. These places are so incredibly tiny, and with such a meager stock, that it is obvious that the proprietors could make but a few cents profit per day.

There was a large open common market, and there we bought several dozen eggs. It was necessary for the buyer to provide his own packaging materials for purchases here, but we had been advised to bring along a handy basket.

A number of cans of fruit were also purchased, and here occurred our one dietary mistake. The fruit on the labels looked delicious, but upon opening the cans we encountered a food familiar only as regards texture—the color and taste was completely unlike anything we had ever encountered. Each different fruit tasted unlike the others, but none of them resembled anything we had ever known. After several tries we gave up, and presented the remainder to friends in England—after warning them of the contents.

We discovered a simple way of pleasing the English-speaking Azoreans. These invariably were anxious to practice this knowledge, and we of course were happy to reciprocate.

We would say, during the course of the conversation: "How long did you live in America?"

Practically none of them had, but we would then say, "You speak English very well."

This always resulted in highly pleased looks, sometimes accompanied by deprecating gestures.

Of unusual interest was the manner in which various bulky objects would be carried on the head with apparent ease and gracefulness. Men as well as women were thus employed, although the latter appeared more numerous.

All the elderly ladies were invariably clad entirely in black—we wondered just what was the precise point for the adoption of these accouterments, but did not get around to obtaining this particular knowledge.

The ladies in general ran to the somewhat solid side, and apparently had little contact with the modern beauty salon. Clothing had small relation to the up-to-the-minute styles we were used to seeing on the streets at home, and it was obvious that they did not resort to certain beauty aids which save Nature the trouble of growing what can be instantly added.

Yet these females were attractive, and we tried to decide just why this was so—making all possible allowance for the fact that we had all been womanless for some time.

Then it dawned—these unsophisticated dears were attractive because they WERE unsophisticated. They seemed so honest in not being ashamed to appear as Nature had actually made them. It was most refreshing! When a shapely one was seen she was doubly admired because you could be quite certain that what you saw was genuine.

In this old-world atmosphere, however, you seldom saw an attractive girl without a hostile-eyed mother close at hand. The girls thus protected flirted shamelessly—their obvious joy increasing in proportion to mother's rising choler.

Some of these girls were indeed pretty, although in such cases their teeth generally did not match the remainder of the presentation.

A damsel at the telegraph office was a veritable doll, and we spent some time inquiring for messages we were not expecting. There was a serious language barrier in this case, but we enjoyed the confusion.

A similar situation was encountered at the hotel in Plymouth, although there was no language difficulty here. The girl in question operated the telephone switchboard, and seemed to have a perfect genius for plugging into all the wrong connections. This was doubtless frustrating to the people actually telephoning, but as she was beautiful we forgave her—willingly.

CHAPTER 15

One disappointment at the Azores was our inability to find replacement batteries for the major lights we had. These used a large cell which was easily obtained at home. At Horta, however, the only obtainable batteries were the small varieties which are usually used in the average flashlight.

We had been using one of the larger batteries in our compass light, but it had now run down. The difficulty was remedied by our use of two tiny kerosene lamps which we had on board. The Skipper had seen them advertised by a ship-fitting concern, and had bought them as decorations, as the cost was but a dollar or so each. They proved invaluable, and we forgave them the rings of soot which they deposited overhead.

When leaving America we had not expected to make any landings prior to our arrival at England, and so the stop at Horta presented some questions in the department of the exchequer.

George had no money of any kind, Bill had about thirty U.S. dollars, while the Skipper had a nest egg of $200 in travelers checks which he had been hoarding to pay for provisions for the return trip. George and Bill had money waiting for them in England, which was of little aid in the Azores.

An interesting development awaited us when we visited the local bank. The Skipper's travelers checks were cheerfully and speedily changed into the local currency, escutos, while Bill's American money was refused! Something to do with rate of exchange, apparently, and he was advised to go to some nearby business establishment. We did, and the transaction there appeared simple enough.

Steamer day occurred during our stay, and the ship entered port early in the morning. We had not planned to meet it, due mostly to the time of its announced arrival. We were awakened by the first of a prolonged series of explosions caused by fireworks. Here was a surprise. These people would certainly use any excuse to celebrate. Well, if that was the way things were done here, we would act the same.

As we went to breakfast we heard a military band marching down the street in full voice. We leaned out a convenient window, as the dining room overlooked the thoroughfare. Not only was it an impressively large musical group, but their uniforms were splendid.

Following them came groups of townspeople dressed in their best, and a festive air was much in evidence.

We enquired of the one waiter who spoke a little English, and discovered that this was not the usual steamer day, but that the band which we had just seen had won a national contest while in Portugal, and had brought great honor to Fayal. It seemed that it was from a tiny nearby village, and if they could obtain that many players from so small an area, musical talent must be common here.

We later heard a guitar band (plus one violin) which played some splendid music. We were told that the reason there was no music in any of the coffee houses was that because of the night life on the Island of Terceira, where the American air base was located, all unusually talented performers decamped to the lure of big money.

Apparently many of the local residents were anxious to make a more personal acquaintance with things American, for there was much talk of the many material advantages of living in the United States, but apparently it was quite costly for the average Azorean to leave his country. To the ones who did actually emigrate, the hurly-burly of modern America must appear frantic indeed after the calm of Azorean life.

An interesting conversation was held with a shoemaker, through the medium of an interpreter. The workman sat on a hard stool, and the only evidence of his trade were a few scraps of leather and other oddments. It was quite a contrast with the modern American version of this business.

We had sought out this craftsman because Bill was anxious to find a pair of sandals like the ones which a few of the back-country people wore. This footgear had soles made from the tread of automobile tires, and the design was so completely functional and basic that the overall effect was nearly pure art.

103 TRANS-ATLANTIC TRIMARAN

The shoemaker was in turn quite interested in learning how his craft was practiced in our Native Land. As he listened and talked he was busy sewing a new pair of soles on some battered shoes. He plied his needle industriously, pushing it through the thick leather after making the initial hole with a small punch.

His eyes grew wide as we described the various machines used in America, although we had not been in such a shop for some years, we did recall rows of spinning wheels, with varying surfaces for different tasks.

He finally held up his two work-scarred hands and said, "This is a Portuguese machine."

CHAPTER 16

Having arrived June 1, it was evident that we would miss the start of the Slocum Race, which was to begin June 11. However, there was a grace period of two weeks, so we still had time.

On the evening of June 6 we reluctantly cast off, with a goodly proportion of the population of Horta on hand to bid us farewell. We were anxious to make a flashing departure, for the local paper had publicised the fact that our "curiosa embarcao" was capable of a thirty-knot speed. These people were too polite to publicly express their doubts as to the veracity of this statement, but obviously were there to see for themselves.

There was but a light breeze, but the assembled people evidently took that fact into consideration, and were obviously amazed at the way we dashed through the calm waters of the harbor. A half-dozen camera enthusiasts were awaiting us at the far end of the breakwater, and to the accompaniment of clicking of shutters, we sailed into fading light.

The wind fell calm, and we drifted for hours. We had thirteen hundred miles to go, and were making an inauspicious beginning.

As we slowly coasted between Fayal and the neighboring Island of San Jorge, which lies just NE of Pico, we encountered a reef stretched

Two happy mariners. George and the Skipper look as though a meal has been announced.

across our path. We were drifting rapidly toward it, and with no wind for propulsion, were most upset, especially as there was no reef shown on the chart, which we checked repeatedly.

"Boy," said someone, "if that isn't a reef it must be tidal action, but it sure does look like a reef."

Sure enough, it was a tide rip, and after a few gentle curtsys in deference to its presence, NIMBLE drifted through it.

As darkness pressed upon us, an Easterly wind arose, and our craft flew through the water, which had become quite choppy.

This wind was approximately Force Four, and was practically the only moderate breeze encountered on the entire trip. The Atlantic Ocean is a mean, nasty, illogical body of water. This point of view is the result of our one journey, of course, but any of us would gladly give it an opportunity of revising this opinion.

"I know how they arrive at those Force Four arrows on the Pilot Chart," said George, "the wind is either Force Eight or Force 0, which averages out to Force Four."

In the light of our experience, this did seem a logical explanation. Not only did the strength of the wind differ from the indications on the charts, but the direction of it was also from everywhere except where shown.

We had heard tales of how unfriendly is this body of water, but we frankly did not believe all we had heard. After all, it was Summer, and we were bound to get some favorable conditions sooner or later. Bill had sailed from Bermuda to England, and had encountered 2,000 miles of favorable SW winds.

We had been counting on winds from this direction, but on the entire journey encountered SW winds but for two days, and on each occasion it was so rough, with the swell from NW, that we jogged along as slowly as possible under reefed jib.

How is it at sea on an ultra-fast boat? Well, you can skyrocket across the seascape at twenty knots or so, but the bouncing about becomes monotonous because a strong wind engenders rough water. This does not apply on down wind courses, however, for then the rate of progress is nearly limitless, if the waves are sufficiently large. To sail on courses other than down wind at great speeds would require a much larger trimaran, which would make the waves smaller in proportion to the size of the boat.

Impressions of this boat's speeds are magically intensified while lying in one's bunk.

With the sea but a planking thickness from one's immediate area, its whispering, rushing sounds appear overwhelmingly close.

The greatest impression is one of continuous acceleration—faster, faster, and ever faster!

NIMBLE slides across a wave which builds rapidly under her. The feeling is that of a fast elevator—up—up.

The boat starts to surf, feeling as if rocket propulsion has been added—the upward movement halts, to be immediately replaced by a headlong dash—forward and down.

The wave has broken, and NIMBLE shudders as she whisks through the foam—riding like a fast train on a strangely irregular but somehow soft roadbed.

The feeling of acceleration grows and grows—up, forward and down — up, forward and down — up, forward and down—water is rushing with incredible speed past the slicing hull with ever-increasing rapidity; overwhelming the senses—denying reality, faster—faster—faster!

It can be tolerated no longer, and the berth occupant claws his way into the cabin, expecting to see the waves going by at supersonic speed.

But no—the pilot chair is squeaking softly as the man on watch lounges, slumped back on his spine, steering with his feet on the wheel.

The sea is indeed going by rapidly, but at the normal pace—a silken, darting advance through the water.

You grope for something to say—something to mask the overwhelming unreality of the infinite acceleration you have been experiencing.

"How's it going?"

"Fine—want some coffee?"

"No, thanks."

And so, back to the bunk, this time to sleep, with the rushing, swifting noises fading into nothingness.

CHAPTER 17

The welcome breeze which wafted us from Fayal lasted but a few hours, and our fare henceforth was light and variable zephyrs.

We had a distance of 1,300 miles to go—the direct route was somewhat shorter, but we had to stay well away from the Coast of Europe in order to avoid the Portuguese Trades, which sweep Southward along the coast below England, and which could prove a definite handicap should we encounter them.

We sailed due North, and had planned to turn directly East when we reached the proper latitude. Besides, with our watch newly corrected before leaving Horta, we had no navigational worries, although it would have been handy to have had a radio direction finder in case we encountered fog toward the end of our journey.

Three days before reaching England, we encountered our last gale, and for twenty-four hours were back in the old routine, running with reefed jib alone.

The wind in this case came from the SW—we actually had a fair wind at last—good old prevailing SW! Alas, it built up so quickly that we soon must reef.

The water was amazingly rough at first, for with a strong SW wind and the prevailing NW swell, we were taking a beating.

A beating in a trimaran is apparently different from a beating in an ordinary boat, however. Many times the Skipper would turn and look at two cans resting on the polished surface of the rear crossarm. A can of cleaning powder and a tall, narrow can of detergent remained in place—mute testimony to the actual ease of motion. These were upset only three times on the journey when crashing waves from the side knocked the crew from their feet.

Through gale after gale, glasses, cups, etc. left on a flat surface would remain where placed. If you wanted to pick one up, you just reached to where you had put it down—and there it was.

Although the motion of NIMBLE is far less than conventional types, she does of course conform to the slope of the particular wave upon which she is riding.

This slope could be steep, but in actual practice is not noticeable unless the horizon is being watched.

The reason for this is that the movement felt by those on board is a produce of acceleration— you feel only a lifting movement as the craft rises, and a downward thrust as it descends. There is no danger.

Our crew was convinced that their craft was non-capsizeable before the passage started, although they had not yet been in outright storms. It makes no more sense to go to sea in a capsizeable boat than it does to go to sea in one which can sink. Both situations are unwise. Also dangerous is a boat with poor maneuverability, which may not be able to get you out of a tight situation.

An incident emphasizing the non-capsizeability of NIMBLE as encountered on the trip.

On this occasion, the boat had been driven far off course by storms, and it was desired to regain the proper heading as soon as possible. Even though the waves were still mountainous, they were not all breaking. It was, however, a reckless decision, made early in the trip, when a fast passage was sought.

The boat was being sailed across a particularly steep sea when the Skipper suddenly realized that she was heeled so far the mast was almost horizontal—much farther than ever before. Just as he had a chance to become really frightened, the wave crest above the boat broke, and tons of water cascaded over the vulnerable craft! The impact threw the helmsman out of the pilot's chair and to the floor, where he lay helplessly, eyes on the transparent hatches, which were now covered with swirling white water.

He lay waiting for the color to change to green, signifying that the boat had turned turtle, and that the voyage, and even life itself, was coming to an end.

The appearance of the water did change, but instead of the color green, it was the same old leaden sky, and the boat was sailing merrily along. After that experience, there was never one moment of doubt as to NIMBLE's stability.

Our SW wind continued to build, and soon the swell changed direction, so we had the pleasure of not only a fair wind, but a following sea, as well. We were sorry that the breeze did not increase to a major storm, for then the waves would have been sufficiently large so we could have made some remarkable time.

We had long since abandoned the hope of making a fast passage, but were still wishing for some outstanding day's runs. We had hoped for at least one 400-mile run in twenty-four hours—this is not yacht time—this is time achieved by only a few of the greatest clipper ships. We would have settled for several consecutive three-hundred-mile days.

Such was not to be, however, and all we had was a Force Eight breeze which at least was from a favorable direction.

You might think that for a tiny sailboat to travel 400 miles in a day is fantastic. It might be, but is nothing compared with a plan of the Skipper's, which he expects to fulfill within the next several years.

His goal—ONE THOUSAND miles per day in a sailboat! You might consider this impossible, but it is not illogical when you hear him explain how it will be accomplished.

It is all based upon the movement of waves. The ones we encountered in the Atlantic, for instance, are said to travel at a speed up to thirty knots. We know that NIMBLE will surf indefinitely on one of these, which makes her speed over the bottom thirty knots, as well.

The difficulty with the Atlantic brand of waves, however, is that they will run for a while, and then subside. The whole process must then be repeated with a new wave.

"Well," you might way, "how can you go a thousand miles per day under those conditions?

113 TRANS-ATLANTIC TRIMARAN

Even if you could stay on one wave at thirty knots, that's only 720 miles for twenty-four hours. ONLY 720 miles?"

That is not a bad figure for a starter, but we have heard that the waves in what is known as the Roaring Forties at the bottom of the world make the Atlantic brand of comber look kindergarten size.

These hurtling mountains of foam in the Forties, it is said, sweep undisturbed around the entire world at a rate exceeding forty knots, and one individual wave is said to persist indefinitely! Now you get the idea.

In the light of NIMBLE's performance on the Atlantic, the Skipper believes that it would be a relatively simple feat. Even if a wave could not be ridden indefinitely, some completely unprecedented distances could be covered.

NIMBLE would be suitable for this purpose—it could even be done in one of our twenty-four-foot NUGGETS, which we have mentioned can be built for $600 (this was in 1960).

However, the Skipper wants to build one trimaran larger than NIMBLE — he thinks that thirty-five feet would be about right. You might say that size doesn't seem much different from NIMBLE's thirty feet, but in boat language it is— some seventy per cent larger. The reason for this is the manner in which volume increases, and when you build a boat you are just enclosing so much volume. If you make a craft twice as long and twice as wide as another one, you are only doubling those dimensions. The volume, however, increases by the cube, or two times two times two —so the volume becomes eight times as great.

He thinks that a boat of this size would be about as large as he would want for himself, and at present, at least, does not contemplate a bigger one. Besides, he has been designing boats at a dizzy pace for five years, and as he has a number of other interests, thinks he might like to spread himself around a bit.

How would this new boat differ from NIMBLE? As present plans go, she would be quite similar, except that she will have a central open cockpit and a second cabin aft. The rig will be yawl—a large mast forward and a smaller one aft. One of the principal reasons for the yawl rig is that it will present an opportunity to have a stay-free rig—at least on the mainmast.

A mast without stays has many advantages, but on a multihull with tremendous stability it would be a difficult engineering feat to construct such a spar, especially if the boat should be kept simple for the amateur builder.

Instead of ordinary side stays, his new boat will have combination side-back stays. These will run from the ends of the second cross-arms to the top of the mainmast. The mast will swivel 360 degrees, and the amount of swivel will be controlled by the boom.

When the automatic-release cleat lets go in a squall, the sail will be free to flog down wind on any heading, removing pressure from the rig. On other boats, the boom runs free until it engages the side stays, and if the wind is from astern so the sail is pressed against these, presure remains.

Not so in the new design. There will also be a companion sail to the mainsail, which will be set

115 TRANS-ATLANTIC TRIMARAN

opposite, acting as a spinnaker, or an overgrown pair of staysails. With the free-swinging booms, these may be set forward of the transverse, if required, and should be a tremendously versatile arrangement.

With this rig, chafe is eliminated, meaning that sails should last indefinitely. In speaking of chafe, we might mention the system used in the NIMBLE voyage. This consisted of a claw which slid along the boom. Wherever this spar happened to be set, a line from the claw pulled the boom downward. This can be done relatively simply in a boat which is very beamy. The result is that the sail is straightened out, giving more effective area, and it cannot belly forward and chafe upon the stays. The new system, however, should be far more effective, because in the arrangement just mentioned, the boom cannot go too far forward, or the stays will be encountered.

How will the new thirty-five-foot LODESTAR look when she is doing forty knots?

It is not difficult to envision clouds of spray, screaming wind and crashing sea, with sailors dressed in oil skins and with haggard faces, lined by weariness and fear, struggling with their last puny efforts to keep their bark afloat in an unequal struggle against the overwhelming forces of Nature.

Well, the Skipper doesn't see it that way at all, for the wave will be doing all the work, with the trimaran just running smoothly down its face, while the crew relaxes in the cozy cabin.

Assuredly there must be a great amount of wind to develop waves the size he will seek, but only enough sail will be carried to keep the boat going.

It might only be the equivalent of the reefed jib. We won't know until we get there.

And so, perhaps the boat will be doing only about ten knots through the water, but will actually be making the same speed over the bottom as is the wave itself.

If you are a surf-rider, you are probably now all agog with excitement, for we have told only half the story.

The last part has to do with quartering a wave, instead of running directly before it. The greatest speed on a surfboard is not made when running directly before it, but by quartering, or going across it. When you run before a wave, your board (or trimaran) slides rapidly ahead, and then slows down and appears to almost stop as it starts up the back slope of the one ahead.

When the original wave catches up once again, and the board climbs higher and higher, until the wave steepens to the point where gravity prevails and once again the board is dashing swiftly ahead. Thus the overall progress is not smooth, but a series of pulses.

Our voyage in NIMBLE also showed that it was possible to run so fast down the face of the wave that the sails would come aback when the wind speed was exceeded. This may not be too objectionable, but is not smooth sailing.

Quartering the wave is another matter entirely. The slope moves smoothly ahead, at a steady pace. If you run directly before it, your speed will be exactly that of the wave. If you run across it, however, the speed you achieve across the face must be added to the forward component of the wave, and the actual distance traveled will be that

TRANS-ATLANTIC TRIMARAN

much greater.

Although the Roaring Forties waves are reportedly huge, their shape may not be suited for surfing—which means that the faces must be sufficiently steep so that gravitational pull is available. As far as is known, they have not been assessed by a surf-rider, so it looks as though the Skipper will have to go and find out for himself. Of course, under storm conditions, they must steepen over the normal configuration, and perhaps a howling gale will be needed to make a run of the required distance.

It is now planned to seek these waves at the conclusion of a South Sea voyage which is contemplated within the next few years. If desired conditions are found, it will take only a few days to reach Cape Horn, and it looks as though our next voyage will find us on the East Coast of South America, unless we hop over to Cape Town.

CHAPTER 18

At nidnight a screaming rain squall arrived from the NW, and in ten minutes that huge sea was completely flattened, with small waves going in various directions. It fell calm shortly after the squall.

We had become tired of squalls at night—even after calm days—and had developed the habit of automatically reefing down at dusk, rolling the mainsail down about eight feet. It was a wonderful, secure sensation, for with our easily-driven boat the speed seemed to hardly diminish, and there was no impression that the boat was feeling even severe gusts. The mainsail would remain reefed until after breakfast, which could be as late as ten o'clock in the morning.

We were now enveloped in a dense fog, and for the last 450 miles of our trip could not get a sight. Of course, we also had no radio, no log to tell distance, and no fathometer. All we had was George, our navigator, to whom we cheerfully transferred all responsibility.

We would drift along, and then say, "Which way, now, George?" Or, "Tell us when to turn, George."

Our wrist watch was of course accurate, so we could tell our longitude—if we could get a sight. Our latitude also depended upon such an accomplishment, for we now had no means of telling when we should head East.

Although we had no log, we had developed the faculty of making quite accurate guesses as to approximate average speed, and hoped that this accomplishment would aid us in our current situation.

Of course, if we headed East and just kept on going, we were bound to hit Europe somewhere. As both George and Bill spoke several languages, all we had to do was ask the first person we met some questions, and we would have a good chance of discovering our whereabouts. However, we were aiming for Plymouth, and naturally wished to reach there first.

It was fairly certain that we were close to our goal, for through the all-enveloping fog came multitudinous ship's foghorns, and we blew our little mouth-power device so enthusiastically that it soon ceased to function.

As the fog sometimes thinned momentarily we could see trawlers at work, but never were close enough to enquire directions.

Darkness was descending—we were just ten days from the Azores, and should have travelled the needed distance.

George ceased figuring for a moment: "We should reach the Lizard in about two hours—it should be dead ahead."

We had great confidence in our man, but Bill and the Skipper accepted the statement with reserve, although neither said anything.

Just then we spied through the fog a small Dutch freighter travelling the same course we were holding. We edged his way so that our headings would intercept. We hailed the bridge and asked the captain the location of the Lizard.

"Fifteen miles, straight ahead." He waved in a friendly manner as mist separated us once again.

What a relief!

As we advanced a new note was added to those of ship's horns.

A siren! Sure enough, it was the Lizard.

The boat by this time barely had steerage way, and according to the overwhelming sound of that siren, we couldn't have been more than several feet from the source of that tremendous noise. We remained in the same location the balance of the night, apparently held by an adverse current.

And so, here was our landfall, and the statistical part of our voyage was over. We had sailed 3,800 miles in 28 sailing days. Our daily average worked out to 135 miles, which is about twice as fast as an ordinary boat our length would have gone under similar conditions. We had not had a chance to display our boat's great speed, but were satisfied, none the less.

Our good overall time was not a tribute to NIMBLE's potential (top, 30 knots), but to her light weather capabilities. In ghosting and light air conditions this craft will move as fast as the wind itself, as long as it is not from ahead.

There are few glassy calms, and a movement of air is all that is required—she will do several knots with the sails hanging limp, regardless of her modest area of 325 square feet.

This was emphasized when we put over the rubber dinghy for some fun before reaching Plymouth, and discovered we had to row like mad just to keep even, although NIMBLE was apparently becalmed.

And becalmed we were — this time a glassy calm, at that, and it took an additional twenty-four hours to sail the fifty miles from the Lizard to Plymouth.

At that time we had several queer visitors. The approaching sight was mystifying — first would come a round black dorsal fin about six inches high, followed at several feet by a disembodied scythe-like object in the vertical plane, beating back and forth in a deliberate, rhythmical manner.

It was a strange vision—until we realized that what was beating was the tall tail of the selfsame fish which sported the dorsal fin. We were later told that what we saw were basking sharks.

Although still enveloped in fog, we did receive a visit from Old Sol, and had the opportunity of a relaxing day in the sun. We had no drying of gear to do, however, as nothing had gotten wet on our leg from the Azores.

CHAPTER 19

As we approached Eddystone Light near Plymouth, we could hear the fog signal—it was the booming of an explosion, which was a novelty for us. Every five minutes it would sound, and perhaps being somewhat light-headed from the nearing completion of our journey, we would look at each other and grin: "Missed us again!"

As the Skipper came on deck just before dawn the next morning, there was George still navigating. He had been up all night. The strain in the fog was beginning to be felt, and perhaps the accumulated tension of the past several days was adding up.

"Say, Skipper—there is a low-flying aircraft with one big light around here — and it doesn't make a sound!"

"I just got here in time," thought the Skipper, "our boy is well 'round the bend."

It seemed that no one was at the helm; NIMBLE's wheel was hard over, and she was spinning around in the fog—jibing, filling, and then jibing again. The compass card was whirling like a top. The low-flying aircraft was actually the Eddystone Light.

George refused to turn in, and although his reputation as a navigator was already secure, he insisted on maintaining his vigil.

NIMBLE fog-bound in the English Channel. This is the only condition in which she was reluctant to sail.

He pointed excitedly—"There's a Nun buoy!" Then he added, "Never mind—it just flew away!"

This called for an explanation. There was a small black flag attached to a stake on a fisherman's float. When first mistily seen, it was hanging in the shape of a Nun buoy, but a subsequent breeze caused it to flutter, making it look like a pair of wings.

A land breeze was building, and soon NIMBLE was tearing through the still water, although close-hauled. George was shouting in glee.

"We must be doing eight or ten knots," said the Skipper.

"Eight or ten!" came a voice from below, "I can't miss this."

And so up came Bill, and we all sat around, enjoying our little sail, for speed in a fast sailboat is probably the most exhilarating kind there is, with overtones of skiing and surfriding.

It might seem strange that after 3,800 miles of sailing, it was still so much fun. As a matter of fact, as soon as we entered the harbor, the crew wanted to sail around instead of berthing. We were proud of our ship, and wanted people to have a look at the boat of the future.

It was later decided to berth at Millbay Docks, which are protected by locks, and so escape the eleven-foot local tides.

As the Skipper was making these arrangements he could feel his crew glaring at him, and knew what they were thinking—with locks—you can't go sailing whenever you want!

Plymouth Harbor has an interesting breakwater. It is free-standing across the harbor entrance, with neither end touching the shore.

125 TRANS-ATLANTIC TRIMARAN

The man on watch in the control tower was flashing a light signal at us. We felt like fools, for we had failed to bring along reference material which would have enabled us to decipher his message. Anyway, we did have flying our ensign and the quarantine flag.

On the East end of the breakwater was an interesting structure, consisting of a metal meshwork ball atop a steel tower. This was described in the Coast Pilot as a rescue chamber, with a capacity of six men. Apparently it was for refuge when waves were dashing over the sea wall.

We had since lost the land breeze, and drifted past the breakwater, headed for a spot marked on our chart as the quarantine anchorage.

We had furled the sails and were getting the anchor ready when we saw a handsome motor boat approaching. It was that of the Port Captain, and we were given a tow to his area; to remain until cleared by customs.

CHAPTER 20

Previous to our arrival at Plymouth we had read all of our available literature describing this area, and it was exciting to realize that we would actually see places where much of our history and heritage developed.

As we approached the quarantine area we could see evidences of ancient fortifications, close by urban developments of the most modern type.

The low mound ahead was the Hoe, the historic place where Drake was bowling when notified of the arrival of the Spanish Armada. The story goes that he replied, "Gentlemen, shall we finish our game?" and then went out to decimate the hostile fleet.

Also here were the Mayflower Steps, where our forbears descended to the small boats which carried them to the famed Mayflower. We saw these, as well.

Plymouth had been badly bombed during World War II, and we had been wondering if any evidences yet remained.

There proved to be but a few such grim mementos, scattered about, but Plymouth proved to be a revelation. The entire heart of the city had been rebuilt in the most modern manner—a unified functional collection of handsome buildings and beautiful malls and parks. This stretched for

George decides to speed things up while becalmed off Plymouth.

many blocks, with new construction rising on every hand.

It was hard to imagine a more attractive arrangement, and we missed only the familiar traffic lights. Here it proved to be an apparently deadly game of who dares who as pedestrians and automobiles sparred at every crossing. Perhaps our long absence from such scenes made us unduly apprehensive.

In the meanwhile, we had been sitting at the dock, waiting for customs to clear us. They were just across the waterway, but apparently their boat was busy elsewhere. Bill had dashed up town in order to get to the banks before noon, as it was Saturday. He would pick up enough cash to carry us until we could get better organized. He was also anxious to discover the whereabouts of his wife, who came to Plymouth to meet us a week previous. He did not know where she now was.

The customs officers did not arrive, so the Port Captain volunteered to drive us around to their office in his car. That automobile ride was a rude reintroduction to civilization. The car shot around a blind curve, ignoring a "Slow Down" sign. To make it worse, we were on the wrong side of the road! It would have been the wrong side in America, at any rate, but this mental adjustment takes some time to become effective.

We arrived at Customs just to see their boat headed away, bound for NIMBLE but several hundred yards away. A bit of telephoning took care of that, and the launch was soon heading back.

Meanwhile, we had been receiving reports on the preparations and the actual start of the Slocum Race, which had taken place one week earlier. We still were well within the two-week grace period, however.

The insular people of England are far more interested in boating than is the average American, and the publicity given this race was extensive. Television crews, photographers, and journalists in large numbers had swarmed about the boats for days, and the most minute detail of equipment, supplies, and personal trivia were eagerly displayed to the waiting public. A number of newspaper accounts had speculated on our possible arrival in time for the Race. In typical newspaperese, none of them said WHEN NIMBLE arrives—they invariably said IF NIMBLE arrives.

Customs formalities were brief, and it was pleasant to deal with people who obviously took pride in their work, and were as courteous as possible. The same applied to immigration officials who checked our passports. It felt strange to be classified as aliens, but that was what we were, all right. As for the Bill of Health which the Port Doctor at Horta had refused us—it was not even mentioned!

Next came a visit to the local yacht club, where all our mail had been accumulating for weeks. We had a veritable mountain of letters and telegrams, and it took some time to absorb it.

Some of the news was disquieting—the Skipper had to return home immediately—business was calling. He had a simple explanation, "If I had not neglected the business to build the boat, I wouldn't have to go home now."

There went participation in the Slocum Race, unless Bill or George would like to take NIMBLE.

She was all ready, except for supplies. Their itineraries with families, etc., were already set, however, and they could not spare the time.

Now we had a real problem. What to do with our faithful vessel? Bill thought he might have a chance to get away in a few weeks, and then would like to cruise the Mediterranean for several months. The boat could be sailed across the lower latitudes of the Atlantic in the Fall or Winter, and the Skipper could rejoin her for a cruise to the West Indies. She would later be put up for sale in Florida, as he had already designed a thirty-five foot trimaran he wished to build.

We decided to move NIMBLE to the Millbay Docks, in which tide-free basin she would remain until Bill could return. He planned to enlarge the central cabin so it would extend over the side decks as it does in the standard model. This would give him substantially more living space for the projected cruise.

He thought it a good idea to first sail the boat to Gibralter, and do his alterations in the sunny climate there. It would take only a week or so for the intended work.

The Harbor Master gave us a tow the several hundred yards to the Docks, as it was high water shortly after noon, and the gates would then swing wide.

"Looks like an airplane, doesn't it?" We could hear the voices of the men on the launch discussing us above the sound of its motor. We did not want NIMBLE to act like an aircraft, either, and were alert at the wheel in case the towing boat should suddenly stop. When such an event occurs NIMBLE just keeps right on going,

131 TRANS-ATLANTIC TRIMARAN

and even though it is light in weight its narrow hulls offer practically no resistance to the water.

One thing which amused us was the invariable looks of astonishment when some vessel would ask us to heave them a tow line. Out would go our one-fourth-inch diameter Nylon rope, and they just couldn't believe that such a tiny line would suffice. It not only would, but we would have liked to further confound them by instead passing along one of our one-eighth-inch lines. This would also be strong enough for a tow in smooth water, but we were afraid it would be nearly invisible, and some other craft might attempt to run between us and our tug.

Soon NIMBLE lay in deathly still water, in the precise spot where the Slocum racers had docked. There were many articles of personal gear which we would have liked to ship to America, but here it was Saturday afternoon and it would be difficult to make such arrangements.

Just then a visitor popped up, and we were lucky to make the acquaintance of Ritchie Symons, a local newspaperman who had covered the preparation and start of the Slocum Race. He was more than glad to see us, for apparently there had been so much speculation as to whether or not we would actually arrive that we had assumed a nebulous character.

He was a sailor as well as a newspaperman, and his interest in NIMBLE was so great that we talked for hours about the entire project. Upon seeing him the next day, he said that he was so excited by our story the previous night that he had not been able to sleep until the wee hours of the morning! It was gratifying to know that we could impress one of the usually sophisticated newspaper gentry.

However, we were to learn that practically everyone in Britain is interested in affairs nautical, and a constant stream of newspaper clippings concerning our boat followed us home. A number of people sailed NIMBLE, and their comments were highly flattering. One of the sentences regarding NIMBLE's ability particularly pleased the Skipper. Quote: "Arthur Piver has made the Atlantic Ocean as narrow as the English Channel." He was amused by one headline which said: "Brilliant Design—Or Just Luck?" He knew the answer to that—a lot of darned hard work. NIMBLE was also described as "the smoothest craft afloat," and "obviously the boat of the future." She received an interview (via her custodian) on BBC, and was slated for an appearance on television.

CHAPTER 21

We had moved to a nearby hotel, and as we planned to depart Plymouth the following noon, got in as much sight-seeing as possible. Arrangements were made for Ritchie to ship home the equipment we needed there, so there was nothing to keep us in that area except the strain of parting with our gallant vehicle.

We were to think of her with more than usual affection when we encountered what we hope was an isolated case of taxi driver jitters. This character would scream in demoniacal rage at the slightest thwarting of his intended path, and would turn around hurling insults, meanwhile continuing to drive madly ahead, while looking backwards! This was somewhat more than unnerving, and was a stern reminder that we were no longer of the sea and its comparatively easy (and safer) ways.

Each time this driver would finish a tirade he would smile at us and remark how he really told off that "so and so." We were beginning to wilt from the strain, however, and got out as soon as we could.

The next day found us on the way to London by train, and we enjoyed the sight of the remarkably well-kept countryside, dotted with evidences of long-established structures.

We arrived at our hotel in London. Bill and George had been there a number of times, but it was all new to the Skipper. He thought it was fascinating, with a charm completely unavailable to younger lands.

The young lady at the hotel desk had obviously been too long out in the sunshine. "Say," said the Skipper, "you make me feel right at home, for you are obviously an American Indian."

She looked him up and down, saying in a very frosty manner, "I am one hundred percent Irish, and I just happen to be sunburned. I am NOT an American Indian."

Sad to relate, that was the typical reaction of the English girls we encountered. They just didn't appreciate our perhaps peculiar manner of friendliness.

One of the high moments of our trip was about to occur, for we had made arrangements to visit Doctor John Morwood, who was leading light of the Amateur Yacht Research Society. He lived an hour and a half train journey South of London, and had asked us to spend the following night with him, which was Monday.

We had planned to rent a car and stop at the marine museum at Greenwich on the way down, but this plan was shelved when Bill learned that he had to leave early the next morning for Denmark, where his wife was staying with her family.

Thus George and the Skipper bade Bill good bye—our little assemblage was beginning to break up.

They were anxious, however, to see Dr. Morwood, and took the train to Hythe, Kent, in the late afternoon.

135 TRANS-AMERICAN TRIMARAN

Dr. Morwood and the Skipper had long been pen pals, for the AYRS was founded in 1955, the same time as the start of the latter's designing career.

The AYRS had proven a valuable clearing house for many ideas related to boat design, for actually there had been many amateur designers working independently, who had mostly been just duplicating each other's mistakes, unbeknownst.

It correlated all the various theories, and now an amateur could start with some proven concepts and go on from there. The bi-monthly bulletins were storehouses of new ideas, and it was interesting to compare those of the pure theorists with those of the practical constructors.

The Society had been advocating the catamaran for years, and now large numbers of these boats were beginning to appear, due in large part to the pioneering efforts of that organization.

Hythe proved to be an entrancing little village, and soon the travelers were deep in conversation with their host and some of the AYRS members.

It was strange to meet a man whom you had known only through correspondence, and even though that correspondence had amounted to thousands of words, the actual physical encounter was intriguing.

They kept staring at each other. "So you are John Morwood," or "So you are Arthur Piver." Apparently each was satisfied with the interview.

Of course the English were anxious to hear all about NIMBLE's voyage, and had innumerable questions to ask as to how she reacted under various conditions.

They seemed uniformly delighted at the results, for here again was vindication of one of the

Society's theories—that the trimaran configuration was perhaps the most logical of all for cruising purposes.

One of those present announced his intention of starting to build one of the Skipper's twenty-four NUGGETS, which made the designer happy.

George and the Skipper spent the night at the Doctor's estate, and were awakened in the morning by the arrival of their host with tea—which they gladly accepted as a logical way of approaching a new day.

The Skipper had to dash back to London by train to meet an appointment with the press, while George returned in a more leisurely fashion by automobile with one of the other guests. He had an instructive personally-conducted tour.

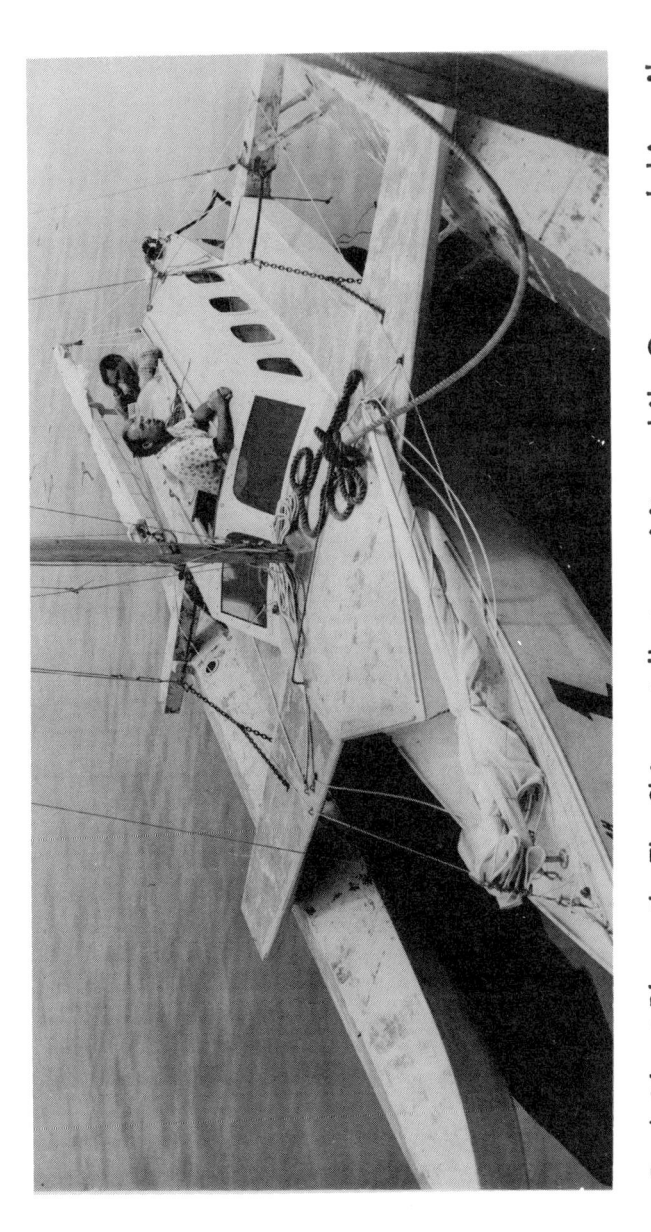

Dockside at Plymouth. The Skipper talks to a visitor, while George reads his mail.

CHAPTER 22

That afternoon the two met for the last time in London; George was flying to Switzerland to meet his family, and the Skipper was due home as soon as possible.

As he flew over the Atlantic, he was struck by the overwhelming contrast of the two modes of travel. The speed of the aircraft was indeed a miracle, but as a passenger he was no longer an individual fulfilling himself—he was only a dull statistic.

It was nice, though, to be able to look disdainfully down upon those annoying clouds which had so long barred the way between those two enamorata of his—the sun and the sea.

He had to stop near Boston to gather his pickup truck, and with two trailers behind pick-a-back, began a lone 3,200 mile journey which took him four days at twenty hours a day.

This was a grind, but he had ample opportunity to think of the fascinating journey just completed, and evaluate the relation of the various individual episodes to the overall accomplishment.

NIMBLE's passage had converted the Skipper, making him a dedicated cruising man. Before, he had only wanted to sail like mad, whooping and hollering in exhilaration, and his little day-sailers had provided all the required thrills.

139 TRANS-ATLANTIC TRIMARAN

Now he had discovered that he could still whoop and holler, having the same sailing fun, and live in comfort, besides.

Not to mention visiting friends in interesting places, and the addition of in-the-flesh friends rather than the ones made just by correspondence, etc.

The most fun in sailing is surfing, and NIMBLE surfed clear across the ocean. She can even surf upwind—she climbs up the face of the sea, and then surfs down its back. Sometimes when sailing across the seas, she would find herself on the apex of the wave, and there would be a choice of surfing either right or left. Many times on downwind courses, she would exceed the speed of the wind itself, so that the sails would come aback.

This ability of sudden spurts of speed, however, has limited the application of the wind vane for self-steering boats of this type. As speed through the water increases, the apparent wind draws ahead, for instance, changing the vessel's course in relation to the vane. When the speed of the wind is exceeded by the craft, the vane is of course useless.

That is the reason why the Skipper did not feel too badly when he learned he would have to fly home immediately after reaching Plymouth, and so must forgo the Slocum Race. He realized that more work is necessary to find the answer to the problem of self-steering without the use of electricity. However, NIMBLE does have great directional stability, self-steering on almost any heading.

What are the ideal characteristics for a cruising sailboat? We believe NIMBLE has them all—

the only shortcomings we have noticed have to do with mooring. In the first place there is the wide beam. This is a joy otherwise, but of course means that you can't get this boat into the usual narrow·berth as found in our modern marinas.

Secondly—when at anchor NIMBLE tends to charge around. This is due to her shallow draft, so that the wind will push her about because of light weight and little bearing under water.

There are those who claim that the ability to go to windward is the least important characteristic of cruising sailboats. We believe this attitude to be completely fallacious. You can't always sail the trade wind routes, and winds do shift. Sooner or later, you will find yourself in a situation when the ability to go to windward will mean the difference between safety and seeing your beloved craft ground to pieces on unfriendly leeward strand.

From our observation we would say that in moderate conditions,. our thirty-foot NIMBLE will go to windward at about the same rate as a conventional fifty-footer. In really rugged going, there is no comparison, for with slicing hulls and tremendous stability this boat will keep going when the usual craft is knocked down flat and refuses to push its massive bulk into foaming head seas and obstructive gale. The inertia of a heavy boat will help it keep going once it has started; when it does become stopped it is doubly difficult to get all that mass moving forward once again.

What about a motor? We believe that the modern cruising sailboat needs one, for there are many situations when just a little power means the

141 TRANS-ATLANTIC TRIMARAN

difference between bobbing around for an extended period or resting comfortably in port.

However, the difficulty with the engine is that your reliance on this mechanism may allow you to become embroiled in a situation where only it can extricate you. The fact that the sailor is certain it will invariably operate has resulted in some wrecks.

We had no motor on NIMBLE's voyage, and did not consider it at all necessary, even though we did drift aimlessly for days in fog. This we accepted as part of the game, and surely the joy at the arrival of wind in our case would have resulted in muchly modified emotion if we had been motoring in the meantime.

In other words, a motor does much to lessen the challenge of sailing, which is one of its greatest charms. We have noted on San Francisco Bay the reactions of some of the sailors there. At the first sign of adversity—down come the sails, and on goes the motor. If it fails to start, the operator is paralyzed with fright. This is adventure?

However, we still think a motor has its place. We are, of course, light-weight addicts, and the thought of a great inert mass of usually unused and highly expensive metal in the bilge, with its attendant danger of gasoline when this fuel is used, is a hazard at least of the mental variety.

Then there is the thought of dragging a propeller through the water. It could be of the folding variety, which would help, but in a fast boat any drag is objectionable, because its resistance rises disproportionately as sailing speed increases.

There are now available through-the-transom propeller units, some of which may be folded so they are above the waterline when not being used. Some may be unbolted and easily removed, as well. This might be a possible solution, with a small engine mounted clear aft. Then there is the outboard motor, which we probably would use because of initial low cost and convenience in mounting.

One of these units opened our eyes when NIMBLE was launched. We wished to tow her to her mooring, which was about a mile from the launching ramp. A friend in his NUGGET offered his services. There was no wind, and so he fired up his little two-and-one-half horsepower outboard, which looked to be the proper size for mixing cake-batter in the kitchen, and we were amazed to see this tiny unit, mounted on a twenty-four-foot boat, pulling a thirty-footer—all at the rate of several knots.

His motor had a geared propeller, which seemed to make the difference, plus the fact that our boats are easily driven.

We believe that a five-horsepower unit would be sufficient for NIMBLE for occasional service. It can be mounted out of sight (and protected) in the side deck, swinging down in the vertical position when needed. We would probably carry but several gallons of fuel, regardless of the length of our projected voyage. The overall weight of this arrangement would probably be only around sixty pounds.

CHAPTER 23

What sort of personality is attracted to the search for solutions to the problems which formerly afflicted multihull boats? These used to include: poor maneuverability, capsizing, sluggishness in light weather, diving of the lee bow, poor directional stability, and pitching in a chop (hobby-horsing).

Apparently the basic requirement is that of a challenge, and the Skipper's attitude toward navigation might give an insight of how his mind works.

In the first place, as navigation is now practiced, it is a simple art. Equipped with the latest in tables (we used H.O. 249), the correct time, and an acceptable result on a sextant reading, anyone who can do simple sums and look up the correct column in the Nautical (or Air) Almanac can work out a satisfactory sight. Of course, he will have to follow a certain prescribed procedure. There are about a dozen necessary steps.

Now this is simple indeed, especially when you compare the hours of complicated mathematics which were formerly required—and which meant that the person of average attainments just did not have what it took to accomplish this essential task.

Modern knowledge, as included in various navigational publications, is now easily available, but do you think this would satisfy the Skipper? It did not, and what do you think is his reason?

"Anybody can learn to navigate with this system. It is only not much of an accomplishment and no challenge, but it's still too complicated, as well. I'm going to work out a better, simpler system."

Here is a man who not only cheerfully concedes he is no mathematician, but the fact that many gifted persons had spent lifetimes trying to simplify this incredibly difficult process meant little to him. He was sure there must be an easier way. He didn't even want to have to use any tables.

And so, he began working out his own system and although he did not perfect it on our one voyage, he expects that it would not be too difficult, if some time were spent on it.

His system requires but three major steps. Here is how it is supposed to work:

1. The Nautical Almanac tells the location of the sun (on earth) at any given moment of the day.

2. The sextant angle can be easily converted from degrees to nautical miles.

3. The direction of the sun from the boat is observed (by compass) when the sight is taken.

If you know where the sun is located on earth, and if you know your distance from it (in miles) and you have the bearing of the sun from the boat, all the essentials are right there.

You mark the position of the sun on the chart, take a reciprocal compass bearing, and measure the number of miles distant from the sun's position on this line—there is your boat!

Of course, it must be more difficult than that, or numberless smug navigators would suffer a

145 TRANS-ATLANTIC TRIMARAN

great blow to their egos. Suppose the sun is so far away (on earth) that its position is not on any available chart? Suppose that an incredibly accurate compass bearing is require? This is not usually available on the average small boat. How do you take a compass bearing when the sun is nearly overhead?

The Skipper just chuckles when these difficulties are pointed out. He considers them completely minor, and believes his system needs only a little development before it can be made to work. Besides, gnomic charts show directions as parts of great circles, and so it shouldn't be difficult to measure your distance from the sun as a straight line.

Of course, a latitude (noon) sight is a simple affair, anyway. All that is required is a sextant reading taken at the point of highest elevation of the sun. The morning or evening position could be found with the Skipper's method. In any event, even if his system were not particularly accurate, it might be used by some luckless mariner who happened to lose his navigation tables for some reason or other.

The Skipper has a similar attitude in regard to the design of sailboats.

"Many people in boating take themselves seriously, but the truth of the matter is that no one knows much about boat design, regardless of the many technical terms he may reel off or the mountains of mathematical data he may produce.

"If a fraction of the money spent on, say, aviation research, were applied to the problems of the sailboat, it would become a science, but at the present moment is actually an art."

His objection to the usual cruising sailboat is mostly a matter of weight.

"A boat is a vehicle, and any vehicle must pay a penalty for excess weight. A heavy boat makes about as much sense as an aircraft made of masonry."

Great weight in a sailing craft (and boats cost so much per pound) causes waves, and this is what limits the speed of the usual boat, so that it can usually go only at a certain slow speed which is related to its length.

Our modern boats, on the other hand, with only a fraction of the same weight per unit of sail area, do not make any waves with their slicing hulls and so there is practically no limit to their speed. With multiple hulls, they possess the ideal sailing combination of great stability with little weight.

CHAPTER 24

The three men parted fast friends after the voyage, and this is significant. You might think that it would be only natural—persons with shared happy experience should be friends.

However, it is a well-known fact that after having been thrown together in a small vessel, people often become enemies instead of friends, and we feel this new type boat makes a significant difference in this realm.

Basic cause of friction is fatigue, and fatigue is present even in the finest weather aboard the usual sailboat, due to the endless rolling, together with having the craft often heeled at an impossible angle.

Those who have fought to move about below in these boats when severely heeled can report on how unbelievably complicated it can be. Everything which is at all moveable becomes one sodden mass in the lower lee corner of the cabin, and this must be walked upon when moving about— there is no other place to step, although some have reported as having walked on the actual side of the boat, rather than the floor.

Continued, severe rolling has plagued boats for centuries, and in the days before metal stays the very masts could be rolled out of the ship. The following story, in which the Skipper was a participant, featured an extensive display of this nautical gyration.

A party had been cruising to Alaska, and was nearing the home port of San Francisco. A severe storm had arisen, and everything seemed to go wrong. First the main gaff on the eighty-six-foot schooner snapped aloft in a wild gale. This tore the mainsail to a severe degree. Then all the other sails blew out. There was an attempt to start the motor in order to obtain some control over the vessel, but this failed.

Then the ship started to leak. With the motor inoperative, the usual engine-driven bilge pump was of course of no use. There was a small hand pump in the cockpit floor, but this yielded a discouragingly small stream of water, accompanied by the necessity of a considerable amount of energy needed to produce that. It was decided to send an SOS, but the storm had also damaged the antenna. A man offered to go aloft to repair this essential bit of gear. By this time the ship was rolling both rails under, and he had a difficult time climbing to the cross trees, sixty feet above the deck. At the end of each roll, just before the ship started the return movement, there was a motion aloft like the cracking of a whip, and the

man was unable to do anything but just barely hang on—he was unable to free one hand to do any work. He could hold on for but a period of several rolls, and had to return to deck—he was lucky to get down safely.

Now the ship had drifted close to some coastal rocks, and because the sails and motor were of no aid, it was decided to use a small motor launch

Very first sail was made in light conditions.

aboard to tow the vessel offshore.

The small craft was launched with difficulty due to the rolling, which treatened to smash it against the side of the mother ship. It got away successfully, however, and was able to pull the vessel to seaward for several hours.

An attempt was now made to get the launch back on board, but it proved impossible because of the continued rolling.

By this time, some small sail had been made, and the ship was making a little headway before the monstrous seas. As the launch was an expensive one, and indeed only three months old, it was decided to tow it, and a long line was attached.

Suddenly someone glanced astern and excitedly pointed, "Look at that!" The launch was surfing down the wave astern, headed for the schooner!

Luckily it just missed, passing with a swish of spray and stopped about mid-way past the ship, which was now headed uphill on the back of the next wave. Everyone watched the launch as it then slowly moved astern once again, wondering if what they had just seen could possibly happen again. It could! The tow rope tightened momentarily, and the boat again started surfing, dashing toward the now thoroughly alarmed group which watched its flashing approach with dread.

It missed again—this time on the opposite side. The Captain said not a word; he stepped to the cleat, cast off the tow rope, and the launch drifted astern. It was never heard of again.

In the meantime, the schooner sank lower and lower in the water, while the crew worked frantically, wearily, endeavoring to at least keep up with the inflow. Below the scene was indescribable.

Water had already arisen above the floor boards, and five hundred gallons of diesel fuel oil had escaped from the tanks, and was mixed with the bilge.

When the ship would roll, this greasy misture would run between the inner skin and the inside of the hull between the frames, and would then explode from under the side deck clear across the cabin.

It was impossible to move about below. It would have been bad enough to attempt travel with water shooting clear across the ship at the end of every roll, but the oil made everything so slippery that there was no chance of having any personal control whatsoever.

The seven men aboard by this time began to eye the remaining life boat, which had a capacity of four. The ship continued to sink, and was already at a desperately low level. One man descended the galley ladder to obtain provisions for the life boat, and a roll hurled him against the sink in the corner. He grabbed a leaden outlet pipe for support, and water squirted between his fingers—there was the leak!

About that time out of the fog came a tiny fishing boat. By paying the operator double what he expected to catch in fish that day, he agreed to attempt a tow. A small port was not far distant, and the little eight-horse-power motor of the fishing boat was able to succor the disabled sailboat—still rolling.

We can mention another incident concerning rolling which is more up-to-date. A year ago a brand-new, beautiful, forty-foot plastic sailboat was cruising down the lower California Coast.

The wind was astern, and this superlative creation of several famous naval architects rolled so badly the crew could no longer stand it, and put in for shelter.

In the same conditions was one of our twenty-four-foot NUGGET trimarans, and its progress through the selfsame waves could perhaps be best described as a sort of leisurely skating.

It anchored for the night alongside the other vessel, which was moored in a somewhat open roadstead, so it was still rolling.

The trimaran sailors were invited aboard for a drink. They did not stay long—they became seasick!

Even in what should be the ideal conditions—running before the trades with the ship steering herself with twin staysails, friction among the crew still continues, for then the ballasted boat rolls madly, as there is not wind from the side to steady her.

The multihull does not roll, due to its great stability and the lack of a heavy keel, which gives a pendulum effect.

In the trade wind conditions mentioned above, NIMBLE can sail three hundred miles (two times as fast as the usual boat of a similar length) per day, with not much more motion than a billiard table.

And so, with the Skipper nearing home, our story draws to a close. He was weary of continual driving but that was only a temporary inconvenience.

Life was exciting and rewarding—and he had dreams to fulfill.

Dreams to fulfill—

APPENDIX

We enjoy discussing boats with the many persons who are interested in our work, and as it has been our policy to freely impart any of the knowledge which we have gained through experience and observation, it is only logical that we share it with readers of this book.

We will begin by discussing the multihull in general, and will then explain the method of construction we use.

Our first multihull was a 16' catamaran, made from a commercial kit purchased in 1953. We had sailed for many years on conventional ballasted craft, and the little catamaran was a revelation— speed and fun and thrills far beyond anything ever before experienced.

The boat had some faults, however, and after we had sailed it for two seasons decided that it could be improved upon; feeling that our lack of any formal knowledge of naval architecture at least prevented us from knowing what could not be accomplished.

These catamaran shortcomings were ones which had apparently always affected this type. Their maneuverability was poor; they capsized too easily; were sluggish in light airs; and were prone to pitching—or what is worse, hobby-horsing. This latter consists of a residual motion which

2 APPENDIX

continues after the wave which caused the original pitching has gone by. We spent some time on a 20-foot manufactured catamaran which was a holy terror at hobby-horsing. The bow, upon encountering a wave, would rise so high the aft deck would actually be submerged, and the boat would keep on pitching, rocking just like the traditional wooden steed in the nursery. A sad, sad, sight—one which unfortunately—and unnecessarily—continues in many of the so-called "modern" catamarans.

The secret of non-pitching and non-hobby-horsing is to have generous bearing aft. As the bow rises, tending to depress the stern, buoyancy aft at the water line or slightly above prevents the stern from being depressed.

Also, the buoyancy of the bows should increase slowly as immersion progresses—a too full bow will throw the forward portion of the boat abruptly into the air. On our boats, we have relatively high, narrow bows, which have enough buoyancy so the bows cannot be run under—even when flying down a steep wave, but the stems must be deeply immersed before the full buoyancy is effective. In normal choppy conditions, these bows are so fine they merely slice delightfully, possessing just enough buoyancy to rise to the waves without pitching but not actually diving through them.

In our trimarans, the bows of the floats have a comparatively long overhang, so they must be deeply immersed before the considerable buoyancy near the deck is utilized, moving the effective buoyancy forward as the float is driven more deeply into the water. This is a principal reason it has been found impossible to drive the bows of

3 APPENDIX

these boats under.

There is a reason for full bows in many modern multihulls, but this reason is related to poor design. Some of these boats have the tendency to bury their lee bows when driven hard, and in order to prevent this, the buoyancy of the bow is kept full, thereby causing too much lift forward, resulting in pitching. The solution in this instance is to move the mast aft a few feet, and the bow-burying movement simply disappears, as the thrust is absorbed by the boat's natural stability.

Our first design (in 1955) was the 20-foot PI-CAT, which was the first of the modern American catamarans, with semi-circular hulls and twin boards—one in each hull.

This boat was a success, and although she did not have full bows, the beam at the water line was carried well forward in order to prevent the bow-burying experienced with our first catamaran. We sailed the first boat clear out of sight on a half-dozen occasions because the lee bow would depress until it was skimming the surface of the water—when a steep wave would appear, the bow would keep right on going—down! It wasn't dangerous, as the boat would merely stop abruptly in a cloud of spray—when the sheet was released, it would back out of the water, and then away she would fly once again, spouting water from every scupper.

Our new boat did tend to pitch in extreme conditions, although she did not hobby-horse, so several years later we built the 17-foot fiberglas PI-CAT, which had a very fine bow, with a hollow entrance, tapering to a V to a semi-circular midships section to a flattish transom.

As a small day-sailer, this boat did not have a high bow, but a flare at the deck line reduced spray and kept the boat—through dynamic action—from driving under even when sailed full speed down the face of breaking seas.

This catamaran broke the maneuvering bottleneck as she could come about so fast that the crew had to actually hurl themselves across the craft in order to be on the proper side when the sails filled on the opposite tack. Observers who saw her maneuver for the first time frequently shouted in amazement.

As regards maneuverability, the essential factor is to get the ends of the boat out of the water, so when it pivots at the center point it is not pushing vertical planes through the water at the bow and stern. Secondly; the hull sections must be rounded so this water will flow easily past them as they sweep around. Some boats with flattish sides thus have a built-in anti-maneuvering factor.

In order to get the ends out of the water, the underbody must have a definite amount of rocker, being deeper in the center. A rounded hull also has minimum wetted surface in relation to displacement, and is thus faster in light airs.

Some designers are afraid of rocker, as they think it makes boats hobby-horse. Our boats—at least our trimarans—have lots of rocker, and they don't hobby-horse at all. They don't even pitch, as explained above, and they maneuver beautifully.

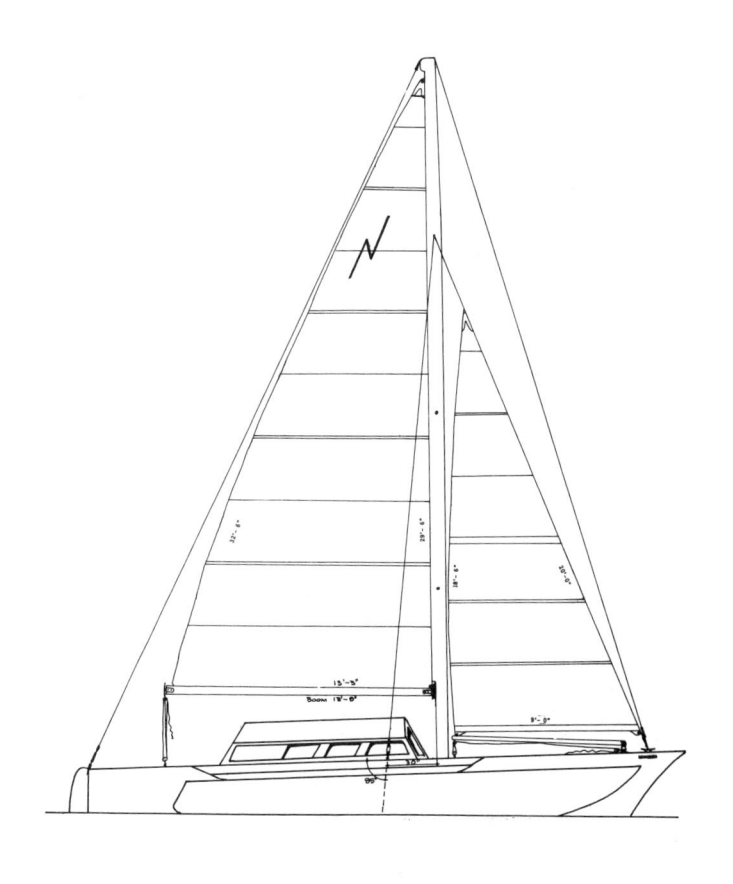

30 X 18 X 2' Trimaran NIMBLE

6 APPENDIX

We seem to be getting progressively less rocker in our day-sailing catamarans, however, for with pure speed machines, straight bottom lines seem to be the most effective.

We have designed what we consider some intriguing twin-hulled speedsters. In general, designers have learned to build superlative small moulded craft of this type, with sleek rounded lines which completely outclass the product of the average home builder. Unfortunately, these boats are fearfully expensive.

We have developed a system whereby ordinary sheet plywood may be easily bent in compound curves, and apparently speedy catamarans can now be home built for a small fraction of the cost of manufactured craft. This saving, however, does not include such expensive incidentals as metal spars, boards, and rudders. We usually employ wood for these components.

One great feature of these high-speed boats is that, for the first time, yacht racing becomes a fascinating sport for the spectator.

The general public previously took little interest in a contest in which contestants moved slowly through the water—but frequently would go off in different directions (when beating to windward) so that there seemed little point in watching a boat sail all by itself.

All that is changed with the zipping multihulls —so far mostly catamarans, which go so fast that everyone—even the spectator—is thrilled.

The first effective display of this sort which we witnessed on San Francisco Bay occurred in 1959, where the Pacific Coast Multihull Championships were held.

7 APPENDIX

We had taken our 17' PI-CAT catamaran to Southern California the previous Spring, and were disappointed with the prevailing light airs in that section of the country.

"Wait 'till you get up North," we told our competitors, "we have some excitement when sailing at home."

And so we later did—too much excitement for some of the sailors, and PI-CAT once reached what must be the greatest speed ever made by a sailboat on water.

A diversified selection of multihulls attended the Championships, and there were some monohulls too, as we opened the affair to any type boat.

The first morning race was completely un-San Francisco-ish—a flat calm.

A Malibu outrigger found it somehow possible to move in the apparently non-existent wind, followed by a 20' CAPER trimaran, leaving the rest of the boats just sitting there.

The afternoon race, however, was an entirely different story. The wind was fresh, with most of the gusts around 40 knots—with others even stronger.

PI-CAT ran into trouble just after the blazing start. One tiller broke off close to the rudder, and the aluminum tube connecting the two disappeared into the depths.

This forced the Skipper to steer with only one tiller, making it necessary for him to always remain on one side of the boat.

These sensitive racing machines require every once of available ballast on the windward side, so with one man to leeward the progress to windward on one tack was poor in comparison with normal sailing.

By the time we had gone once around the course we were in fifth place—as we rounded the windward mark, the leading trimaran CAPER was almost a full leg ahead of us; WILDCAT and COUGER were half-way to the next mark; and SHEARWATER III was a few yards in advance.

Just then a simply tremendous gust struck and PI-CAT leaped not only ahead, but up as well—there were only several feet of the central hull area in the water, with the remainder of the boat apparently air-borne.

We went by SHEARWATER as if she were anchored, and so great was our speed that we rounded the next mark in company with WILDCAT and COUGER. This means that our speed was just double that of these fast boats, and as they were traveling at the rate of about twenty knots—ours was, in terms of sailboat performance—astronomical!

After we rounded the mark, we came upon hapless CAPER.

It is nice to pass one's competitors, but as CAPER was our design, and had been well ahead, we of course wanted her to make a good showing.

However, the wooden blade of the pivot rudder had broken, and Fred was hanging over the transom desperately trying to hold it in place by hand.

"I can see why Fred is hanging over the stern," said the Skipper, "but why is Andy hanging over the bow?"

We later discovered why—Andy was seasick, and every time Fred shouted, "Pull in the jib!"—his crewman would answer—"Shut up!"

9 APPENDIX

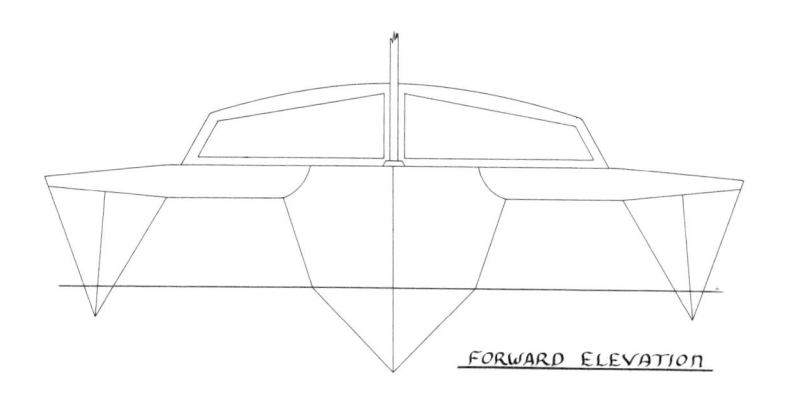

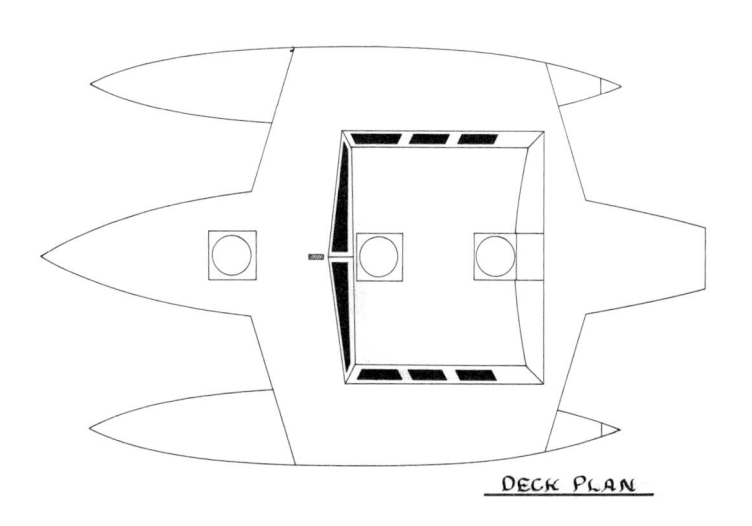

FORWARD ELEVATION

DECK PLAN

Views of Standard Model NIMBLE.

10 APPENDIX

Final standings for the Regatta were: 1. WILDCAT; 2. COUGER; 3. PI-CAT; 4. SHEARWATER.

Several of the racers from Southern California said that they wouldn't be back—the wind was too much for them. The MALIBU outrigger had capsized twice, but it didn't seem to bother her crew —they accepted it as part of the fun.

To get back to maneuverability—we might tell you of our experience in this realm when we first launched NIMBLE. The rudder was mounted and given the first tentative movements. When it was turned, the bow of the boat would swing in the opposite direction—as if the rudder were geared directly to the water.

Only the lightest and handiest of dinghies have such a reaction, and we knew that this boat would have maneuverability which would be outstanding.

Right then the name of the craft was changed; from the tentative MIRAGE ("because people won't believe it even after they see it") to NIMBLE, as the former name was too insubstantial, and now not sufficiently descriptive. Besides, what other multihull designer would have the nerve to call his creation NIMBLE?

Another indication of her maneuverability occurred when we had the identification numbers painted on the bow of the central hull. The boat was being held between two floats, and when the sign painter wanted to work on the second side, he asked that the boat be moved in a complete circle. There was a man at each end of the boat, and each pushed. The craft spun right around— just like a top! It was an amazing sight.

Because of this maneuverability some people think that perhaps this boat will not have much directional stability while sailing. The opposite is true, instead, for she acts as though she is fastened to a taut wire when sailing. The three hulls just tend to run straight, and this boat, because she heels little, does not change her underwater shape as does the conventional boat. Also, in the latter type, the fact that the center of effort of the sails is out over the water (when heeled) tends to give a differential thrust which turns her into the wind.

One thing which delighted us with NIMBLE was the apparent fact that in these larger craft, centerboards are not needed. Even when driving hard to windward, the board could be moved by hand, showing that there was practically no pressure on it. When sailed without the board, however, she did develop a weather helm when sailing fast. This meant that in this boat the board was only a trimming device.

In the many NIMBLEs now building, we are going to use three small fins instead of the centerboard. One will go just ahead of the rudder, and should prevent development of weather helm. There will be a small fin on each float, which will increase lateral resistance at the proper points, but none of them will project beyond the bottom of the keel, so the boat's two-foot draft is not increased.

We have always disliked centerboards anyway. They were difficult to install, the cases tended to collect leaks or worms, and occupied the best part of the accommodation. We had a final discouragement board-wise with NIMBLE when we were at the Azores.

12 APPENDIX

We had beached the boat on a beautiful, mild day to do some maintenance work. The crew had to go to town and the Skipper stayed on board. All at once a storm arose, and as everyone disappeared in the sheets of rain which suddenly appeared, the Skipper had to push the boat out by himself. The water deepened rapidly, and he had to throw out the anchor a short distance from shore, as the wind was blowing the boat toward a rock breakwater, which was now only about ten feet to leeward.

There was so little water that as the waves dashed in, NIMBLE would pound on the hard sand bottom. Of course the board was up, but every time the keel would hit the sand a geyser of water flew out of the top of the case into the cabin. It appeared with such explosive force that he could not stop it, and spent the afternoon and night bailing away.

We will, of course, also eliminate the board in our new 35-foot trimaran LODESTAR, which is now building. With this boat, we not only reaffirm the fact that the high cost of yachting is a myth to the person capable of simple carpentry, but have apparently solved the housing shortage as well. Although we have not completed the design of the interior, it looks as though about eight persons could sleep in the wing section alone. The rest of the boat will be devoted to clear comfort, including a separate cabin aft, and a shower. We estimate it will cost between $3,000 – $4,000 (for materials), and we expect to have not only a luxurious yacht, but a comfortable mobile home, as well. What kind of house could you have for this price—not counting the land?

13 APPENDIX

As far as the question of stability in multihulls is concerned, the solution is merely greater beam, for the amount of beam determines the area of sail which may be carried. The beam must be effective, however, which means that the boat should not have an exaggerated amount of freeboard, for instance, which gets the rig so high above the water that the heeling moment is increased.

We of course like to sell completed boats as well as kits and partially-constructed vessels, but our first feeling is for the amateur builder. Of course, it is nice to be able to pay cash for a boat, but the man who drives every nail with his own hands, and has to sweat to find the wherewithal to buy his materials, derives a personal satisfaction from his completed craft which is simply unobtainable in the bought product.

We know that a man with the initiative and resourcefulness to build his own boat has the qualities which will make a success of almost any venture for which he uses it.

One field in which we do encounter some problems is our sometimes difficulty in convincing people of the importance of light-weight—especially in the smaller boat sizes. The long narrow hull, although very fast, is relative inefficient when heavily loaded, because the wetted surface increases disproportionately. Wetted surface is the chief cause of sailing resistance—not counting wave formation.

These boats often seem to fly—and this similarly must be remembered, as a light boat reacts as does the light airplane—overload it and performance suffers.

This overloading problem seems to be most prevalent with our 24-foot NUGGET, as it can be used for cruising, and many people evidently expect that it can be loaded with all the impedimenta which are usually found on a 40-footer.

We must say, however, that we could appreciate the cause of one instance of overloading when two men returned to California from Mexico with practically the entire boat, including the floats, stuffed full of cheaply-bought native liquor.

We attempt to forestall this condition of occasional overloading of NUGGET, however. The stern is kept relatively narrow, and although a broader stern would give greater buoyancy, if that were overloaded the wide transom would create a great deal of drag, spoiling the boat's sailing ability. Even with the transom well immersed, NUGGET still goes like mad.

In the larger boats, overloading is less of a problem, due to the proportionately greatly increased volume of the hulls. In our voyage aboard NIMBLE, we could see no lessening of her speed, even in the lightest weather. We had aboard supplies for three men for forty days.

In at least our experimental boats, we always seem to have full-length battens in our sails, and people want to know why—especially in a cruising boat like NIMBLE. Actually, the standard model of NIMBLE does not have long battens, which would

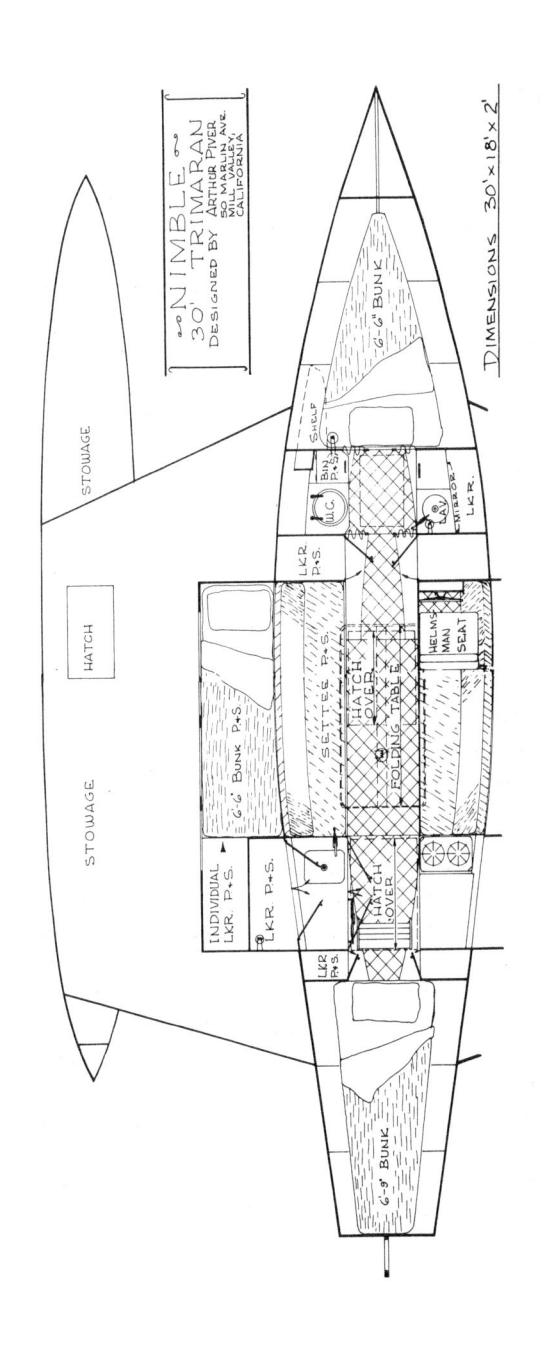

Accomodation Plan-- Cockpit on aft deck optional.

be superfluous as we cannot have a large roach (after curve) of the mainsail, as we now use a permanent backstay.

NIMBLE #1 had no permanent backstay, with a large roach—which is one of our pet likes, as we feel it offers more efficiency in sail shape, plus more area with a lower center of effort on a mast of a given height.

One reason for the battens on NIMBLE was the fact that we thought we had the batten problem licked. We used fiberglas fishing rods, and the action was beautiful—the whippy ends went close to the mast, where the sail curve is greatest, and the butts were at the trailing edge (leech) of the sail, where the stiffness is needed.

These battens were arranged so they were parallel with the boom, and as they were round, and of small diamater, they could be rolled right up along with the sail when reefing.

However, we broke all the battens at sea—with the exception of some polyethylene rods in the jib. As battens are a necessity with our remote jib reefing, we will continue to use them in this sail. As a matter of fact, any jib mounted on a club may be converted to this system of reefing. At a point half way up the luff, have two grommets inserted at the leading and after edges of the sail in the horizontal plane. In the forward grommet, mount two blocks, and the reefing line terminates at the after grommet, following threading as shown in the jib drawing. Two of the plastic rod battens may be inserted in the lower part of the jib to help confine the unused portion of the sail when reefed.

We used five-eighths-inch diameter battens, and the reefing line was one-eighth-inch Nylon. Of

17 APPENDIX

course, if you have a heavy boat, you will need stronger line. For occasional sailing, this reefing system is a bother because of all the line hanging around when furling, but when cruising, with the jib set indefinitely, it is a Godsend.

There is another reason for battens in the mainsail, even if not much roach is used. This has to do with the sails flogging when the ship is head to wind. Battened sails do not flog, but sway gently—it is a delight to be able to overcome the traditional bother and danger of slatting sails. We expect to use the plastic rod battens in the sails of our new boat. These battens are not early so stiff (at the outboard end) as our former fiberglas fishing rod battens, so perhaps the sail will still flog. We won't know until we try them out.

We are sometimes asked, when a discussion brings forth our declaration that we consider the semi-circular bottom to be the best shape because of minimum wetted surface, why we do not use this form on most of our boats.

Well, when we first started selling plans in 1957, all our experimental boats had round bottoms, made with strip planking, with plywood above the water line. Strip planking is actually a simple way in which to construct a boat, even though many small pieces are used. The strips are nailed and glued one to the other, so it ends up as virtually a single solid piece of wood.

However, it does look complicated, and we never could get any amateurs to even try it, and as a consequence did not sell any plans until we transferred to the V-bottom as we now use it.

18 APPENDIX

The V shape is simple to construct, of course, and although we had some reservations as to its efficiency as compared with the former round shape, received a very pleasant surprise when our new boats with the V performed just about as well. We use lines modified about the 90-degree V, which gives the minimum wetted surface for a given amount of displacement of a V hull.

One of our most significant discoveries is the fact that a hull need not be needle-like in order to be fast. Our newest floats are indeed slender, but we have made our central hulls wider and wider, until in our present line of boats there is a comfortable amount of room inside.

Multihull designers previously believed that a hull which was wider than one-tenth of its waterline length simply could not be fast, and it is flattering to see all the new trimarans emerging which use our formulas of length to breadth.

The construction of our boats continually amazes experienced sailors, and is a reason for their occasional initial skepticism.

The structure does appear very light, at that, but here is the reason.

In the first place, of course, there is no heavy keel to have to allow for, which greatly reduces strains. We engineer the stresses so practically all of these are confined to the cross-arm-wing area. Thus the central hull does little but keep the water out, and the floats merely do their lifting function.

The mast is stepped on the cross-arm itself, and thus no thrust need be transmitted to the central hull structure.

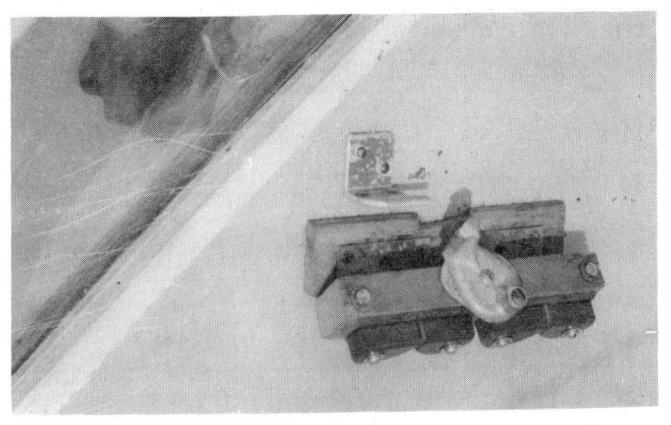

Crude model of automatic sheet-release. In lower view device has tilted after tension unit releases-allowing sheets to pull up and out of cam-action cleats.

Another advantage of having the mast stepped on deck is that in case of rigging failure, the mast merely goes over the side, and does not break as it would if it were stepped through the deck.

Our boats are largely plywood, as this appears to be the most logical material for the amateur builder. It is inexpensive, strong, and durable. Even less expensive grades may be utilized, if protected by fiberglas.

We are fiberglas addicts, but in a reserved manner. This material has many virtues, but it is also expensive as well as heavy.

We design the boats so the plywood alone has sufficient strength, and the glass is added only for waterproofing and for a more permanent finish. We usually glass everything, but in general use such light glass that it weighs little more than paint. The cloth is applied so there are overlaps at the chines and keel, giving additional protection at these important points. A glass shoe is also applied to the keel, as these boats have the great advantage of being easily beached.

As far as the simple structure of the boat is concerned, we use light-weight boatbuilding wood for the framing. In our home locality the only acceptable wood which is at all reasonable in price is Douglas Fir (Oregon Pine). This is satisfactory in kiln-dried stock, vertical grain. We also use it for spars, as it is fifty per cent stronger and stiffer than Spruce, with little additional weight, at a fraction of the cost.

The larger spar stock is not obtainable kiln-dried, so we must use air-dried. Most dealers

21 APPENDIX

consider their wood air-dried if it has stayed out overnight, and we have found we must check the moisture content or the lumber may be impossibly heavy.

Our masts are a good example of our approach to boat building. For instance, a professionally-made conventional spar for our 24-foot NUGGET would cost several hundred dollars. We make ours from $10 worth of solid 2 X 6 Fir. The wood part may be completed in an hour, and we end up with a better mast than the professional one, because of sounder staying.

Not only is such a mast inexpensive and simple to build—it weighs no more than a hollow one of the same size. This is a real puzzler to many people, but here is the answer. In designing these masts, we allow ourselves only the same amount of wood as would be used in a hollow mast. This results in a plank spar, but our staying furnishes the required lateral stiffness, while the long fore and aft dimension gives admirable strength in that direction.

A plank mast is relatively inefficient, aerodynamically, as compared with a round one, for instance, but if they are fitted to revolve, as are some of ours in our racing multihulls, they are more efficient than other shapes when looking into the wind.

In the cruising boats, however, we ignore this factor, as our boats go like mad to windward, anyway.

Designing the mast of NIMBLE was an engrossing engineering problem, for because of the way in which volume (and weight) increases, we still wanted a mast of no more than two inches in thickness. The wood we located was actually only one and seven-eighths inches, and that makes a pretty thin mast in a thirty-six-foot height. We used 2 X 8 inch timber.

In this particular spar, because of its length, some method of stiffening, in addition to the usual triple diamond staying, was required. The mast would be laterally stiff at the spreaders, but would tend to buckle between spreaders, a tendency increased by the fact that we keep our diamond stays taut.

As can be seen in the mast drawing, the answer was to scarf the mast between spreaders, as scarfs as we use them are great stiffening factors. We do not use the traditional boatbuilding scarfs, which require much skill, but put them in the opposite, simple way—through the two-inch dimension. The timbers are merely laid on two saw horses, marked across on a slant with a straight edge, and cut through the thinner dimension with a hand power saw. The joints were then glued, and as we had only a few clamps, we glued one joint per day. Cost of the wood came to $21 for the entire spar.

We expect to use the same system for the mainmast in our new boat, but it will be more complicated because all the stays will go to the masthead, which will swivel. In order to better support the center of the mast, which will have a longer stayless span than in NIMBLE's mast, we will lengthen the central spreader.

In our smaller trimarans, we use some solid cross-arms for simplicity, but in the larger ones such members would become ridiculously heavy.

23 APPENDIX

We thus use aircraft-type box spars, built of plywood. In some of the more sophisticated models on which we are working, the wing structure itself acts as the cross-arm.

We used roller-reefing gear on NIMBLE's main boom, and think it great. The necessary mechanism is quite expensive, however, so we made our own. A drawing is furnished to show how it works. The principal item, the eight-inch-diamater wheel, was bought at surplus for twenty-five cents—it is the handle for a large water valve.

Before starting the actual construction of the traditional boat, the first procedure is to loft it—which means that all lines must be laid down full-size on a floor. In only a medium-sized boat, this procedure could take weeks, and was a severe stumbling block for the amateur builder. Perhaps it was necessary for the complex and intricate structure required for a vessel of considerable weight, but as we practice it, no lofting is necessary for our simple craft.

Our first revolt at lofting resulted in what we called our "telephone system." This consisted of designing the boat as a series of straight lines, arcs, and sections of circles. With this method, you could describe the boat over the telephone, and in about twenty minutes the person at the other end would have sufficient information to build the craft—without ever having seen a drawing of it. We seemed to contribute little to the science of naval architecture with this procedure.

APPENDIX

In the present system, we furnish implicit information as to the building of the frames, which determine the final shape of the hulls. We have a device called the Plotting Board, which is simply a sheet of 4 X 8 foot plywood with a line drawn down the center of the four-foot dimension. This line is used as a reference, and it is easy to lay out the frames from the dimensions given; and they all come out square. The sheet of plywood is later cut up and used in the construction.

After the frames are assembled, they are mounted upside down on two wooden rails (the Strongback) which keep them aligned. In most of our designs, the deck is given as a straight line, and the Strongback corresponds to this line. Thus, when the frames are erected at the given intervals, and aligned at right angles to the Strongback, the boat takes shape. Practically the only tool required in aligning the framework of the hull is a carpenter's square, for the frames are erected at right angles to the Strongback in both the horizontal and the vertical plane.

Primary fastener is glue, and we usually use nails to hold plywood, etc., while the glue is setting up. For economy reasons, we can use galvanized nails, at a tiny fraction of the cost of usual boat fastenings. Galvanizing normally lasts indefinitely, but as we fiberglas all outside surfaces, thus excluding moisture, these should last forever.

25 APPENDIX

One place where we do not economize is in the selection of stainless steel rigging, but fortunately the wire itself is not expensive—it is merely the end fittings which run up the cost.

We make our own end fittings, using a squeezed-sleeve process which was developed for the telephone industry. We have several of these compressing tools, which resemble bolt-cutters; and so for the cost of about thirty cents per fitting for a small stainless thimble and the sleeve, we achieve low-cost rigging. These tools can often be rented near various boating centers.

For the tangs which fasten the stays to the spars and the boat itself, we purchase stainless steel in sheet form, and have it sheared to the proper widths at a sheet-metal shop.

The best material for sails is evidently Dacron, although professional sails cost from a dollar per square foot and upwards when made of this synthetic. However, for the person who must watch his funds, it is possible to make satisfactory (though not for racing) sails from a cotton cloth known as Boat Drill. This is strong as well as inexpensive, and sails can be home-made (using a straight-stitch sewing machine) for about one-fifth the cost of professional Dacrons. We don't recommend the home sewing of Dacron, however, as it is hard to handle. Regular cotton sail cloth costs about twice as much as the Boat Drill. Although sailmaking is generally regarded as an occult art, it is not difficult to make your own, following the directions as outlined in any of the several books on the subject.

26 APPENDIX

In general, however, Dacrons are definitely superior to the traditional cloths, and if possible stretch your budget to include these. What some of our builders do is make their own sails, and then, several seasons later when they can afford Dacrons, they sell their old sails to someone building a similar boat, charging just for the cost of the material.

And so, there is our story. If we have inspired you to get afloat and enjoy the tremendous sport of boating—while saving money in the process— we have done our part. The rest is up to you.

Remote-reefed jib. Control line runs along bottom of photo.

NIMBLE under construction at designer's home.

NIMBLE moored to argumentative barge.

ABOUT THE AUTHOR . . .
by Florence Reid

Arthur Piver (rhymes with Diver) is a middle-aged business paper publisher of Mill Valley, California who is confronted with a hobby which has gotten completely out of hand.

A yachtsman all his life, he became interested in high-speed sailing and in 1955 produced his first boat, which led to a bewildering fleet of catamarans, dinghies, and outriggers—twelve of them in five years—with traditional shortcomings of small craft being largely wiped out in the process.

His first design, the 1955 20' PI-CAT, was the first modern American boat of this type, and its features of symmetrical semi-circular hulls and twin boards are now seen on all the latest catamarans.

A 17' version in 1959 once reached a speed approaching 40 knots.

He has produced the first dinghy (16' NUT-SHELL) which can plane when close-hauled to windward (with just ordinary sitting-out by the crew)—a performance formerly considered impossible.

His 1959 10' dinghy SCOOTER has a double-curvature hull which gives great speed when upright but increased effective beam and stability when heeled.

Related inventions — his automatic sheet-

29 APPENDIX

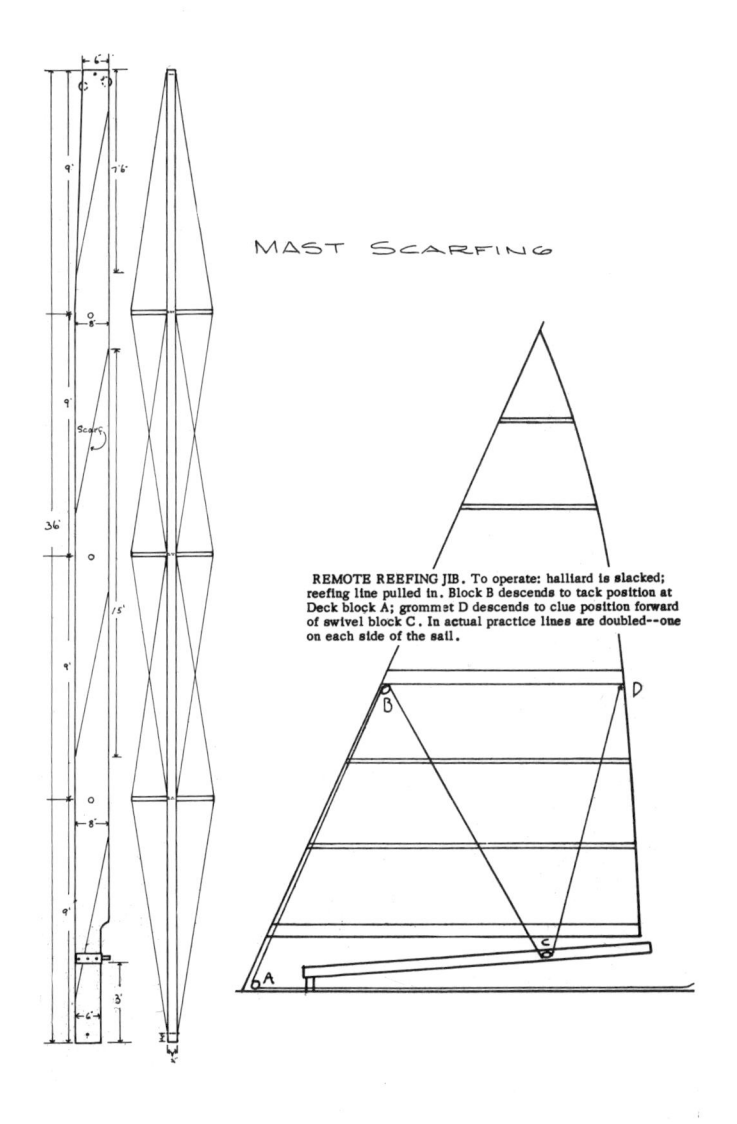

MAST SCARFING

REMOTE REEFING JIB. To operate: halliard is slacked; reefing line pulled in. Block B descends to tack position at Deck block A; grommet D descends to clue position forward of swivel block C. In actual practice lines are doubled--one on each side of the sail.

30 APPENDIX

release and remote-reefing jib—have been declared to be "Godsends" to the cruising sailor.

In 1957 he built his first trimaran (double outrigger) and will be best known for this type.

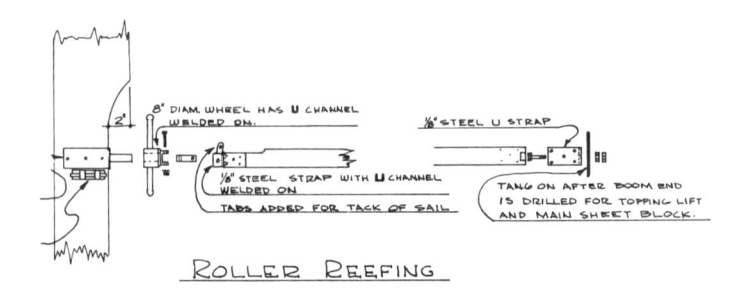

ROLLER REEFING